THE LAST MAN STANDING

Peter Dornan has for 40 years been a physiotherapist in the fields of sporting injuries and manipulative therapy, working with many international sporting teams, including the Queensland rugby team, the Wallabies and the Kangaroos. He has also been an Olympic Games Advisor and Commonwealth Games physiotherapist, covering many different sports.

He is a Fellow of Sports Medicine Australia, and has written two successful books on sporting injuries as well as designing and marketing a video exercise program. For his achievements in sport he was awarded the Commemorative 2000 Australian Sports Medal.

Peter has studied classical sculpture for 30 years and his works are displayed in many prominent Queensland and national institutions, as well as private collections.

In 1997, Peter created a forum for men and their partners to gain support and be better informed in matters relating to prostate cancer. He documented the experience in his 2003 book *Conquering Incontinence*.

Peter has also been freelance writing for some years and has written two factional books, *The Silent Men*, an account of the Kokoda Trail Campaign, and *Nicky Barr, An Australian Air Ace*.

In 2002 Peter was appointed as a Member of the General Division of the Order of Australia (AM).

Peter has been married to Dimity, a speech pathologist, for 39 years. They have two adult children, Melissa and Roderick.

THE LAST MAN STANDING

Herb Ashby and the Battle of El Alamein

PETER DORNAN

ALLEN&UNWIN

Allen & Unwin
83 Alexander Street
Crows Nest NSW 2065
Australia
Phone: (61 2) 8425 0100
Fax: (61 2) 9906 2218
Email: info@allenandunwin.com
Web: www.allenandunwin.com

National Library of Australia
Cataloguing-in-Publication entry:

Dornan, Peter.
  The last man standing: Herb Ashby and the Battle of
  El Alamein.

  Bibliography.
  ISBN 978 1 74114 989 0.

  ISBN 1 74114 989 4.

  1. Ashby, Herb. 2. Australia. Army. Division, 9th.
  3. El Alamein, Battle of, Egypt, 1942. I. Title.

940.5423

Set in 12/14 pt Granjon by Midland Typesetters, Australia.
Printed in Australia by McPherson's Printing Group

10 9 8 7 6 5 4 3 2 1

I dedicate this book to my granddaughter, Matilda Alice Bruijn, and to the memory of her great-grandfather, Captain Dick Crist, 2/2nd Machine-Gun Battalion, 9th Division AIF, a member of Monty's Desert Eighth Army—QX6275.

A Letter from Palestine

A letter from 'The East' it came today,
And all the house is lightened of its gloom:
A sun-browned desert wind through every room
Eddies that bring strange scents of old bazaar:
Of orange-groves beneath the dreaming stars
O'er far Jerusalem. Through these ordered rooms
Where poppies glow; and pale narcissi blooms
Nod in tall vases, sings the desert breeze
Telling of brown battalions overseas.
Khaki-clad soldiers, singing as they go
Along the road to Gaza, and we know,
The very breath of freedom's in the air
With their gay boast, 'Australia will be there',
Mateship and courage, loyalty and truth
The very essence of Australian youth!
We have no fears! Serene in faith we pray
For those dear gallant lads so far way.
AND ONE SMALL WOMAN WALKS WITH EYES A-SHINE
BECAUSE A LETTER CAME—FROM PALESTINE!

Alice Guerin Crist

(Alice wrote this poem while her son Dick Crist was fighting in the Middle East. Sadly, Alice died before Dick finally returned to Australia after serving in the Battle of El Alamein. Dick Crist is Peter Dornan's father-in-law.)

Contents

Acknowledgements

I wish to express my gratitude to a number of special people whose assistance in the preparation of this book was indispensable. First, I have relied heavily on the oral histories given to me by those who lived through the events described.

I am particularly grateful for the personal communication with Zac Isaksson whose advice and paper, 'Key to El Alamein—Trig 29', were extremely important. I have also relied heavily on the battalion history *Tobruk to Tarakan* by John Glenn. Mark Johnston's *That Magnificent 9th* was also very useful, as was Johnston and Peter Stanley's *Alamein: The Australian Story*.

Thanks also to Richard Cameron from the 2/2nd Machine Gun Battalion for his continuous encouragement and editing, as well as Maurie Trigger from the same battalion.

I am also indebted to Murray Adams and David Ryan who helped with editing. A special accolade goes to my patient personal assistant, Carol Jackson, whose comments were always welcome. I am particularly grateful to my wife, Dimity, who was my chief support system and cheersquad when I felt the problems were getting too large.

Thank you also to Ray Hellier for his assistance with maps, and also to Jean Taylor, Doug Tanner and Thelma Hogan for their advice on research. I am particularly grateful for the encouragement of Allen & Unwin staff, especially my editor Catherine Taylor.

Finally, I have to thank Herb Ashby for his patience, openness and willingness to share his unique experiences, to relive all that passed and allow it to be witnessed by succeeding generations. It is well understood that emotions become more vibrant and poignant when viewed through the prism of warfare. Herb's ability to describe a moment in time with breathless urgency and unrivalled intimacy offers insights that are both timeless and universal.

Peter Dornan
January 2006

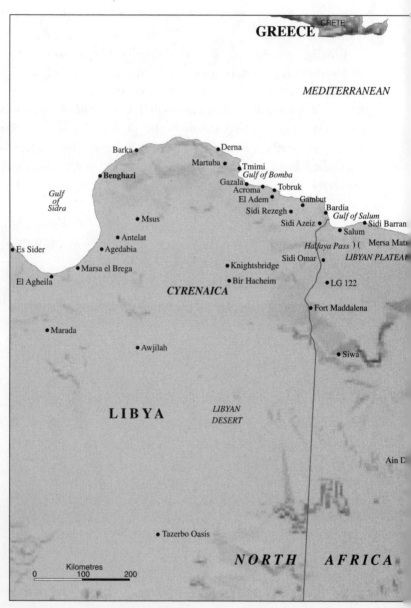

North Africa, circa Second World War

Explanatory Note

This book follows the experience of a handful of men who were part of the 2nd AIF (Australian Imperial Force). The 2nd AIF comprised four divisions (6, 7, 8 and 9—the first five divisions were raised for the First World War) of about 14 500 men each, and fought in many theatres of conflict during the Second World War. The story revolves around the 9th Division and one of its fighting battalions, the 2/48th.

In March 1940 the Australian Army adopted a system in which a division consisted of three brigades, each with three battalions, and various support units. The 9th Division was made up as follows:

20th Brigade	24th Brigade	26th Brigade
2/13th Battalion	2/28th Battalion	2/23rd Battalion
2/15th Battalion	2/32nd Battalion	2/24th Battalion
2/17th Battalion	2/43rd Battalion	2/48th Battalion

Unit structures and level of command:

Unit	No. of men	Structure	Command
Division	14 500		Major General
Brigade	3300	3 to a division	Brigadier
Battalion	850	3 to a brigade	Lieutenant-Colonel
Company	140	5 to a battalion	Captain
Platoon	39	18 to a battalion	Lieutenant
Section	11	3 to a platoon	Corporal

Abbreviations

Military terms

Bn	Battalion
Pl	Platoon
RMO	Regimental medical officer
RAP	Regimental aid post
HQ	Headquarters
AIF	Australian Imperial Force
AWL	Absent without leave

Decorations

VC	Victoria Cross
DSO	Distinguished Service Order
DCM	Distinguished Conduct Medal
OBE	Officer of the Order of the British Empire
MBE	Member of the Order of the British Empire
MC	Military Cross
MM	Military Medal
BEM	British Empire Medal
MID	Mentioned in Dispatches

Introduction

The battle of El Alamein is little known to many Australians today. When questioned, most would not be able to say where it was fought, or even which world war it was fought in. And yet the battle was a significant turning point in the Second World War, and it was the men of the 9th Australian Division who made victory possible. Churchill later said of the battle, 'It might almost be said, before Alamein we never had a victory; after Alamein we never had a defeat.'

The name El Alamein is Arabic and refers to a railway station in Egypt. It takes its name from a ridge, the Tel el Alamein—the hill of twin cairns—between the station and the Mediterranean.

The El Alamein campaign took place in Northern Egypt, and the cold statistics are revealing. The entire campaign, from July to November 1942, cost the lives of 1225 Australians. During the final twelve days, Australia lost 620 men. In this final battle, the 9th Division suffered 20 per cent of the Allied Army's casualties of 13560 killed, wounded and missing, though it formed only 7 per cent of the total force of 220000 men. During the overall five-month campaign, the 9th Division received 5829 casualties, or virtually half of its normal fighting strength.

Yet somehow, to Australians, El Alamein continues to be regarded as less important than Kokoda (where 607 were killed in six months) and Tobruk (where 776 died over nine months). Perhaps this is because Australians viewed El Alamein as a predominantly European campaign—our troops were only a small contingent in a vast army, and our role was underplayed by British politicians and generals, keen for a British victory. At the same time, the more immediate Japanese threat on our doorstep, which was being fought on the Kokoda Track and at Milne Bay in New Guinea, was of vital local concern. Even though the 9th Division became famous for its victories at Tobruk and El Alamein, over the following three years of the war the fight for New Guinea and the Pacific Islands over-shadowed the importance of this 'European' theatre. Our immediate military focus was here; our military achievements at El Alamein were effectively suppressed.

Immediately after the war, men (and women) tried to put the conflict behind them and get on with life. The significance of El Alamein was diminished, and the Australian contribution to this campaign has been neglected in the popular eye.

There are many remarkable men still alive from this epic campaign, although the numbers are quickly diminishing. This story is a personal account of one man who has allowed us to ex-perience this theatre of war through his eyes. This is Herb's story.

At eighteen years, Herb Ashby lied about his age to join the AIF. Like other adventurous young Australians from his country region, he sailed to the Middle East and was thrown into the reality of war during the siege of Tobruk. Though wounded, he survived the conflict and went on to take part in the El Alamein campaign, where he was highly decorated for valour.

Herb's willingness to share his story is testament to his desire to ensure that the sacrifices that war imposes and the trauma it inflicts on individuals is never forgotten. Hopefully, Australians may gain a new appreciation of El Alamein and develop some pride in the role played by our forefathers.

Prologue

Western Desert, Egypt. Not far from El Alamein Railway Station. 23 October 1942.

In the desert, night closes quickly. Herb Ashby had been tense all day and he was grateful for the refreshing coolness. The heat haze, which increases in the hottest part of the day, had been playing tricks with his eyesight, creating a shimmer and causing bushes and scrub to appear as pools of vibrant shining light, confusing his perspective and clarity of vision. He knew the coolness would allow for greater acuity. He also hoped it might calm him a little.

In truth though, he knew nothing would calm him on this night. How could it? He was never calm on the eve of battle, particularly now with his new responsibility. Herb had risen quickly through the ranks, and was now acting sergeant in 17 Platoon, 2/48th Battalion, Australian Imperial Forces (AIF). The previous evening he had been given his platoon's instructions and objectives for the imminent battle, and, as always with these revelations, his stomach had immediately tightened into a painful cramped knot.

Herb had only turned 21 a fortnight ago, and had already been through two major campaigns—Tobruk and Tel el Eisa. In a deliberate attempt at distraction, he wrenched his mind back to his recent birthday party, which he had really enjoyed.

At the time, he had been recuperating behind the lines at the 7th Australian General Hospital (AGH) at Alexandria, which had been set up in a large tent.

When Herb joined up, three years previously, he was lean and fit at 12 stone (76 kilograms) and 5 feet 11 inches (180 cm) tall. When he came down with dysentery, his weight dropped to below 9 stone (57 kilograms). The battalion doctor, Dr Yeatman, whom Herb had known before the war from his home town at Mount Gambier in South Australia, diagnosed him as having 'desert sores in the bowel'.

On 9 October, the day before his birthday, Herb commiserated with a friend in the bed next to him; by this stage he had been in the hospital several weeks and was feeling low.

'How's a man? I'm 21 tomorrow. I'll be able to legally vote and have a beer. And here I am in a flamin' hospital bed, miles from home in a stinking desert.'

The next day, there was to be a film showing at the hospital. A screen had been erected outside and the feature would be played at dusk in the half-light in order to minimise the risk of attack from ranging enemy bombers. As such, the images on the screen were often difficult to make out, and there was only time to play one film before the flickering camera light rendered the hospital a potential target.

That morning an attractive nursing sister approached Herb. 'You're doing pretty well—come to the pictures with me tonight.'

Herb smiled. How could he refuse? He had always admired this particular nurse, and it was his birthday, after all.

The frustration of the previous day gone, Herb enjoyed the feature film and the company. He must be improving.

When they returned, to his surprise, all the beds had been moved outside and a dance floor laid in the middle of the hospital tent. His friend in the bed next to him had arranged for one of the other patients, a piano-accordion player who had been a member of an acclaimed band in London before the war, to lead a dance session for a party in Herb's honour.

Somehow, the nurses and patients had acquired a large supply of stout and, even though many of the men were suffering from dysentery, the night developed into a marvellous party. As 'Happy Birthday' was sung by all, Herb was presented with a key made of cardboard with dressings wrapped around it—and a present. Yep, thought Herb, it was a great party.

The doctor, on his rounds the next morning, laughed and said, 'That tested you out, didn't it?' And indeed it had. Fortunately, Herb was on the way to recovery in his general health, and was warmed by the display of friendship towards him.

A few days later, Herb was discharged back to his battalion on the battle line, despite being not yet fully recovered and markedly underweight. He certainly wasn't fit, being generally weak from his stay in hospital and the effects of the dysentery. The measly daily ration of one bully beef tin and one packet of hard biscuits wasn't helping either.

On his return to his platoon, he was greeted with a mixture of warm welcome and surprise, his men exclaiming, 'You're mad coming back now—it's going to be on.'

'What?' asked Herb.

'The big one—the "big attack"!'

Herb always knew this day—this battle, the 'big attack'—would come. And he knew it would be the largest single conflict the modern world had witnessed since the Great War.

The battalion had been in training for some time, the soldiers learning how to jump off trucks at 50 km/h then roll and take up defensive positions away from the vehicles; how to walk in 'attack formation' behind a tank, supposedly moving through minefields. Herb had missed the training and felt a little vulnerable because of it.

Now, tonight, it was about to start. The evening had commenced only a few hours previously with a church service led by Padre Archbold. Herb liked the Padre. He was a Methodist and a Scotsman, and became personally involved in every battle, much to the worry of the brass. Herb reckoned that the Padre had such strong faith that he believed he couldn't be killed. Herb smiled wryly to himself as he dallied with visions of the Padre regularly being restrained from going onto the battlefield.

Herb knew the Padre to be a good man, and he was affectionately known to all, irrespective of denomination, as 'old Arch'. He would often trudge over the sands carrying his 'little black box'—his portable gramophone—to some forward company, squat on the side of a trench, wind it up and play a nostalgic song. The pleasurable moment briefly reminded the men of home and what they were fighting for. From this vantage point, he was also known to deliver a quick homily to the men.

A dubious advantage of going into battle was that the battalion was served a hot meal, which, while sustaining, reinforced along with the Padre's services, the sense of partaking in the 'Last Supper' for the condemned.

Just before 7.00 p.m., the beauty of an almost full moon, rising golden and large above the desert horizon, was almost lost on the distracted men. A few minutes later, the battalion was picked up in trucks and moved in convoy east along the coast road, and dropped a few kilometres away at the assembly point, a small distance south of Tel el Eisa Station.

About 9.00 p.m., after a restless period of milling around and waiting, the battalion began its movement to the start line under the cover of darkness. It was never comfortable, crawling over sand, but Herb was well trained for it. He half crawled, half crouched for about a kilometre, then dug a small trench for himself and waited.

So far, so good. If the enemy knew they were there, or that the big attack was on, they weren't responding.

An eerie quiet lay over the battlefield. From his position Herb could see one of the six tracks which had been constructed leading to the rear area. They were marked with tin signs and petrol cans containing hurricane lanterns, the light shining through holes for those approaching from the rear to identify. He hoped he wouldn't need to follow one of those tracks. He only wanted to go forward.

It was cooler now—a light breeze had blown up from the south—and the moon had begun its rise into the night sky, casting a silver sheen across the desert and threatening the fragile security afforded them by the darkness. Tomorrow night would be full moon, but it was so bright now that Herb noticed a friend shielding his eyes from the glare with a blanket, trying to catch a few minutes' peace.

Whereas the moonlight would enable easier mobility in the darkness, particularly when negotiating a track through minefields (and this night was selected deliberately for that reason by Lieutenant-General Bernard Montgomery of the Eighth Army), the thought nonetheless caused Herb's unsettled stomach to tighten further. He had strong memories of being silhouetted against the rising moon some months earlier at Tobruk, a perfect target for enemy machine gunners. The scars from this transgression were still fresh in his mind.

However, like most of the men in the battalion, Herb's morale was high. He was aware that a great deal was expected of the Australian 9th Division, of which his battalion was part, and there was great satisfaction for the battalion in the knowledge that they had been situated in pride of place for the whole of the Eighth Army. They were to hold the position of the extreme right flank, bordering the Mediterranean Sea.

At this instant, the two great opposing armies battling

desperately for a political and physical advantage—one of the most important of the war—were lined up facing each other in preparation for what they both knew would be a pivotal shoot out. The armies were separated by minefields 8 kilometres deep and 55 kilometres long. They contained half a million deadly mines arranged in horseshoe patterns that Field Marshal Erwin Rommel, the Axis commander, called the 'Devil's Garden'.

The line of minefields extended from the Mediterranean Sea south to rugged hills that formed the lip of an escarpment leading to the unpassable shifting sands and salt marshes of a quagmire called the Qattara Depression. This inhospitable feature lay 200 metres below the hills forming the border of the depression. Its great importance was that it prevented flanking movements of either army.

Montgomery had under his command 220000 men from seven Allied nations: Britain, Australia, India, New Zealand, South Africa, France and Greece. The Axis Army, composed of both Italians and the famed German Afrika Korps, was commanded by the brilliant and so far unbeatable Field Marshal Erwin Rommel, and consisted of some 180000 men. (Rommel's cunning and talent for improvisation had earned him the sobriquet the 'Desert Fox', a title Rommel capitalised on for propaganda and morale purposes.) At this stage, however, and well known to Allied Intelligence, Rommel was sick, recuperating in Germany, and his replacement, General Stumme, was unprepared in his efforts to guess where and when the imminent attack would fall.

Herb knew what the German and Italian armies didn't: that it would begin in 40 minutes, at precisely 9.40 p.m. He knew that, at that instant, the desert front would explode and things would never be the same. In the meantime, though, the sustained quiet was unnerving. Strangely, there were no motors to be heard anywhere. No shooting. Nothing. The drone of the transport, trucks and tanks of the Eighth Army, which had been moving supplies and resources to the start line, had ceased. The weeks of meticulous detailed preparation were over. Herb knew everybody was in position. Occasionally, over the sound of his own heart, he could hear the eerie calls of night desert birds twittering around the camel thorn scrub. He tried to quieten his mind.

Herb's hands were perspiring as he strengthened his grip on his Lee Enfield .303 rifle. He was wound up like a spring. He knew his stomach would settle the instant imagination and fear were replaced by substance and action, but the knowledge didn't really help. He cursed his nervousness. He wondered if the other men felt the same. No one ever talked about it though. Perhaps, like him, they didn't want to give anything away, didn't want to admit to feeling vulnerable. Once started, this sort of discussion could end up by undermining everyone's confidence in one other. Better not to talk about it. No matter; in a few irretrievable and painfully long minutes he would face this fear and would once again be racing into the gates of hell. Only the strong and confident make it through.

His role, broadly, was to follow members of his sister battalion, the 2/24th, which was to move out first. After the 2/24th had cleared its front line for 2 kilometres, the 2/48th was to move through the 2/24th and thrust deep into the enemy's second line of defence.

It was now approaching 8.30 p.m. The seconds ticked away. Few men spoke, this strange silence still hanging over the desert, each man maintaining a constant vigil on their wristwatches. Just as the tension was becoming unbearable, Herb became aware of a distant murmuring sound, the prelude to battle. It began somewhere to the east, behind him, like the overture of a remote pastoral symphony. Within seconds, the sound was moving through the dark towards him, swelling in intensity.

Herb felt a thrill of excitement, his stomach turning over as he recognised the now rhythmic throb to be the humming motors of British Wellington bomber aircraft. These would support the opening artillery barrage to be unleashed in a few minutes. No stopping the juggernaut now.

Within a few heartbeats, the sound escalated to a fearful surging roar as the impressive flight, the largest Herb had ever seen, passed directly overhead. A few of the planes, flying closer to the horizon, were clearly silhouetted by the glare of the now wide, golden moon, hanging low over the desert.

As the planes passed over, moving towards enemy lines and dragging their retreating sound behind them, Herb was once again left in relative silence. It was now about a minute before zero hour. A few seconds before the symphony would blast into a deafening crescendo.

Herb noticed the silent flickering behind British lines of the long-range guns, strangely out of sync with the steady booming that trailed behind a few seconds later. These had opened fire a fraction in advance of the massed field artillery and the bombers to allow for the combined payloads of bombs and shells to land on the enemy in the same horrendous split second.

An instant later, the clock hands swung to 9.40 p.m. and, right along the 55-kilometre front, Allied gun crew commanders screamed the order, 'Troops, fire!'

Close to a thousand Eighth Army artillery guns now fired simultaneously as light guns, 25-pounders, and medium cannons complemented the already firing long-range guns. Herb stared in wonder, torn at the sight. In an instant, the peace and darkness of the night sky was rent asunder. A wall of flame, some flashes more than 20 metres high, exploded from the mouths of the cannons into the night sky. Wide-eyed, he was witness to a pyrotechnic display defying description—one imbued with the potential for unmitigated damage, the like of which few men had ever before seen.

The desert and sky erupted into a panoramic blaze of orange and yellow flame, numbing Herb's senses and overwhelming his vision. He was aware of an internal warming sensation as adrenalin moved to prepare him for action, the innate chemical reaction allowing him some sense of calm and control. He wasn't so much frightened now as excited and shocked at the wonder of the spectacle. Above him he could hear the dreadful whispering of thousands of shells passing overhead towards their enemy targets.

A few seconds later, Herb involuntarily winced and trembled as he scratched deeper into his trench, instinctively protecting himself from the ear-splitting, earth-shattering roar from the myriad explosions that shook the earth. He could only look and gasp in horror at the effect of the paroxysmal force as it reverberated wildly along the entire front line. Herb felt as if he was in the middle of an earthquake, surrounded by a turbulent electrical storm.

He tried to imagine the devastation the shells and bombs would have wreaked on the shocked enemy. Guns, tanks, airfields, communications and men; all trapped and engulfed in the inferno.

Above the noise of the barrage, he yelled to his mate crouching in a trench some metres away, who was similarly awed by the scene, 'I'd hate to be copping that. Thank God they're ours.'

The attack had created tremendous confusion along the entire Axis line. Shells burst among enemy strong points, exploding and igniting vast square-kilometres of minefields, adding to the terror and bewilderment. Geysers of rock, sand and dust spiralled skywards, while some of the hated German 88-mm anti-aircraft guns disintegrated into fragments as they sustained direct hits. Men crumpled everywhere under the murderous fire, dropping dead from the concussion of the cataclysmic exploding shells, their brains traumatised beyond endurance.

Herb distinguished the dull crunch of aircraft bombs from the staccato reports of artillery shells firing some thousand rounds a minute, above the resonant clang of heavy mortar bombs. Within minutes, the air filled with dust, smoke and the choking acrid smell of gunpowder. And another smell too, peculiar and musty, as shells burst and disturbed the ancient desert.

While processing this cauldron of unearthly sensations, Herb worked desperately to calm himself as he knew that soon, when the firing stopped, it would be his turn.

Then there was silence. A few German and Italian gun commanders had recovered from the initial pounding and the odd shell flying overhead, seeking out the Eighth Army gun emplacements, punctuated the night. But Herb's attention was focused solely on two swivelling British searchlight beams as they knifed into the now dark sky. After five minutes, at exactly 10.00 p.m.—zero hour—the powerful arcs swung inward, intersected and stopped, prophetically pointing westward. It was the sign.

As suddenly as the silence came, it went again as the entire complement of the Eighth Army's guns crashed to life. Herb instinctively ducked again as the roar reverberated right along the frontier, seemingly louder than even the first performance. In front of him, he watched as the celestial signal urged his friends in the 2/24th Battalion to move out of the darkness of their start line and into the maelstrom. He watched them advance, 2 or 3 metres between them, at the even rate of 70 metres per minute towards the opposing lines. Glowing enemy tracer shells sailed over the Australians' heads, highlighting a path for them to follow. White and coloured flares threw a ghostly light on the scene, while gun flashes and exploding bombs framed and froze the men in weird staccato patterns. The pageant was surreal. Herb prepared himself.

PART I

Tobruk

ONE

The Early Years

The rabbit jerked its head up, its nose twitching nervously above its cleft upper lip, its bulging eyes focused into the distance as its sensitive ears pricked upright and rotated towards the sound. Herb quickly darted behind a tree then froze. He was upwind of his prey and was confident he was hidden from the rabbit's view. He held his breath.

The rabbit scanned the immediate area, sniffed, then, apparently satisfied, returned to nuzzling the green shoots at its paws. Herb smiled. He'd fooled it. Concentrating now, he slowly raised his .22 gun, steadied the barrel, took careful aim and firmly pulled the trigger. The bullet smashed into the skull behind the rabbit's ear, dropping it instantaneously.

Briskly, he swung his gun around a few degrees, aimed again and fired two more shots in rapid succession, dropping two more rabbits. The gunfire startled the rest of them. The field sprang to life as literally hundreds of rabbits jumped, raced and scattered blindly and comically in any direction.

Herb straightened and moved into the open. Working the bolt action and trigger with lightning speed, he emptied his magazine case after the fleeing animals. Several more rabbits dropped. Some rolled, some jerked, but they all died.

At fourteen, Herb Ashby was a deadly shot. He had to be. It was 1936, the middle of the Great Depression. Herb was one of ten children—number six—and his father simply could not afford for him to continue schooling. So he had left school the previous year, at age thirteen, to go out and start earning money. Rabbits were infesting the land in plague proportions and presented a ready opportunity to raise cash.

The decision to leave school had not unduly bothered Herb. Many of his friends had done the same. He was born in Mount Gambier, a beautiful and fertile South Australian farming community near the Victorian border, and now lived on a dairy farm at Kongorong, about 30 kilometres from Mount Gambier. To Herb, life was simple and generally fulfilling. It was certainly adventurous. In fact, Herb found a degree of fun in the challenge of hunting and trapping rabbits.

In addition to shooting animals, every morning Herb and one of his brothers would work together, setting a hundred traps around the farm. Later that night, they would walk around the trap sites and pick their harvest, often reaping anywhere from fifty to one hundred rabbits a day. The family also bred their own ferrets which were trained to follow the rabbits into their warrens. The boys would then position themselves to either shoot the rabbits or club them as they came scampering out another exit.

It was easier in winter. The seasonal rains would flood the rabbit warrens, preventing the animals from making a safe getaway when chased. The animals were then easy picking as they literally had nowhere to hide.

Herb also owned a favourite greyhound that was so gentle and well trained that he would retrieve a rabbit without bruising it. Not that it mattered. The two boys would then kill it, gut it and skewer it onto a long rail. They would then place hessian screens over the carcasses to keep flies away and tie the ends. Once a week, three trucks would visit the farm and transport the kill to a cold room at Mount Gambier. From there, they would be transported to England, for ready sale.

Herb would be paid four or five pence for a rabbit, sixpence for a couple—a substantial remittance as a packet of cigarettes cost about five pence, not that Herb smoked.

There were other jobs around the place too to keep Herb occupied. His father ran 40 milking cows on the farm that had to be milked twice a day. The running of the farm was dependent upon strong family commitment. When he started out, Herb's father's plan was to have a large family of boys in order to help with the farm. According to Herb, this scheme appeared to work well.

The first of Herb's nine siblings was born in 1915 and, on target, one was born every year thereafter for the next five years. There was a breather for a year, then another baby each year for the next four years. His father's hopes for all boys started out shakily, however. Even though the first born was a male, he was followed by two daughters. Luckily for his father though, Herb's mother then produced seven sons straight.

At fourteen, Herb asked his father how he did that. 'Easy,' he winked at Herb, 'simply changed the side of the bed.' Herb wasn't too sure if that was the real reason, but he let it go, not being very experienced in these matters.

Herb considered his father to be a good man. Strict, but fair, and always governed by 'family first'. Herb enjoyed life on the farm. There were always projects and work to do, to the extent that they were virtually self-sufficient. He would churn butter for his mother, by hand. She used a special method and her butter was always in great demand at the local store in Kongorong and at Fiddlers, a large department store in Mount Gambier.

The experiences of farm life helped to toughen Herb. Particularly field work; ploughing, planting and cutting oats and other grains. It was hard work, managing heavy ploughs and strong draft horses, but he grew to love the equine smell and to savour the newly turned earth. Further, the acquired and necessary discipline was teaching Herb valuable life lessons. He was also growing in stature, and at the end of his fourteenth year, he was strong and tall for his age, and confident enough to apply for a job on the roads.

As it was hard to get work during the Depression, and some of the men with families resented Herb seeking such a position and made their feelings known; they reasoned it should go to an older man. However, the overseer, Frank Kemp, was more interested in getting the job done, and took a calculated punt on the keen young Herb.

The central feature of road-laying was the need to crack rocks with a napping hammer in order to form the road bed. One particular morning a few months after Herb started, a truck deposited a large mound of rocks which had to be crushed by that evening. Two older men who had been particularly vocal about Herb's presence tested him and pushed him all day. As the heavy work and the day progressed, Herb ached all over and developed large blisters on his hands, but he persevered and matched the older men. The effort won grudging respect and a seal of acceptance for Herb, allowing him to go on to work in that position as a valued team member until he was seventeen.

Physically, these were hard, formative years, yet they served to further shape and strengthen Herb's body and character. His forearms and shoulders grew sinewy and strong, testament to his rugged occupation and outdoor life. Beyond work, he was happily experiencing the usual rites of passage of a young man of seventeen in 1939, which generally amounted to attending local dances on the weekends where he and his mates would have a few illicit drinks to get up enough Dutch courage to ask a girl for a dance.

However, all this was about to change. In the early part of 1939, and for some time before, Herb had been aware of potential conflict brewing in Europe. Not that Herb knew much about Europe. He did know, however, that Germany had rebuilt after the Great War and was once again a strong militaristic nation. And that Mr Chamberlain, the prime minister of England, had apparently averted potential aggression by signing a peace agreement with Adolf Hitler, the German leader. Even though this settled most people into believing Germany would be contained, Herb was acutely aware that whatever happened in England was very much Australia's business. In 1939, there was no denying Australia's colonial heritage and bonds.

Herb's knowledge of war was also limited. Some years before, when he was nine years old, Herb had befriended a veteran from the Great War. Even though the man was probably only in his late thirties, he appeared very old to Herb then. The man was trying to manage a poultry farm not far from Herb's father's farm, although he was finding it difficult as he was shaky and nervous, virtually a wreck, after the war. He had been a member of a local South Australian battalion, the 48th, and told Herb of the terrible days of the great breakthrough in France and Belgium during the final days of the war, and often talked emotionally of all the boys who died, many of whom he had known from the battalion.

Herb would listen with some fascination and the 'old' man took a liking to him, rewarding him by giving him some eggs. He also took Herb for a ride in his sulky to Mount Gambier. It was the first time Herb had travelled out of the district, and certainly the first time to Mount Gambier, and he remembered this adventure with some excitement. Later, he was told by his father that the veteran had been suffering from shell shock, and in retrospect Herb realised that, socially, he was very reclusive. Even in 1939, some twenty years after the war, Herb recalls he was emotionally labile and appeared sick, and old for his age.

Though for a while there was still hope that there wouldn't

be a war, the spring of 1939 brought the news that most Australians expected but dreaded to hear. Herb clung to the radio in the family living room as Prime Minister Robert Menzies announced that the country was at war. Hitler had invaded Poland and the world was watching as he stalked France. Menzies's voice crackled from the radio at 9.15 on the evening of 3 September, 'Great Britain has declared war on Germany and, as a result, Australia is also at war.'

The announcement was not greeted with the same enthusiasm as the declaration of war in 1914. The memories of loss in the previous war were still painful, and the hardships of the Great Depression had led many to believe that Australia should never again be involved in a European war.

However, for a country not prepared for war, by January 1940, barely four months after the announcement, a force of one division and its corresponding auxiliary units—20 000 men in total—had been raised and trained, ready to embark to help 'the Motherland'. These were the forward brigades of the 6th Division. These men believed they would be assisting the British Expeditionary Force who were entrenched in France, glaring at the Germans who were concentrating powerful armies on the borders of Holland and Belgium.

Herb was officially too young to join up (enlistment age was 21), and didn't initially feel compelled to besides as it was the prevailing wisdom of the time that the war would soon be over. Over the next few months, the media called this period the 'phoney war', yet by April events were still smouldering and another division was proposed, and very quickly, adventurous men answered the call to form the 7th Division.

For many, though, there was still not adequate reason to get involved 'over there'. However, by June, two events occurred which altered Herb's perspective, and that of many other men. First, the world witnessed the dramatic and climactic events surrounding the evacuation of Dunkirk. This emanated from Hitler unleashing his 'dogs of war' on 10 May, where he successfully used his blitzkrieg tactic: a devastating combination of dive bombers, artillery and tank spearheads, which forced the withdrawal of the British Expeditionary Force to be eventually trapped on the beaches of northern France off the Strait of Dover.

Second, Italy entered the war after dictator Benito Mussolini formed a partnership with Hitler. Mussolini coveted Egypt and moved to fulfil his dream of a North African Italian Empire. Egypt had long been under a British treaty which allowed British troops to be stationed there. It was therefore important for Britain to retain a foothold to protect the Suez gateway as well as oil reserves in the Middle East. As such, the advance convoy taking the Australian 6th Division to Europe found themselves diverted to Palestine in the Middle East in readiness for a confrontation with Italy.

The 'phoney war' was over. By now, Herb could not contain himself any longer. He discussed the situation with his friends, 'What's England going to do?' There was a degree of indignation and a concern among them for England's, and indeed Australia's, potential loss of freedom. Herb conceded that he must join up. While there was a certain sense of adventure in his decision, mostly he was motivated by a need to help 'save England', to 'do his bit'.

Herb was now eighteen. Along with a few friends from the surrounding district, including Wally Shane and Bill Pride from Spalding—a small community not far from Kongorong—Herb rode to the recruiting centre at Mount Gambier.

While waiting his turn for admission, Herb feared his underage status might be a problem. He changed his birth date, cheekily adding five years to his age. In front of him in the queue, he noticed a half-dozen younger individuals who were obviously only fourteen or fifteen years old. He had heard they had taken a train down from the mining town of Broken Hill. While Herb watched, the desk phone rang. The sergeant listened to the caller with interest, smiled and then called out the boys' names. Herb thought, 'They're gone'. And indeed, they were all put back on the train for Broken Hill.

Herb was next. He hoped he would fare better. When the sergeant asked the usual questions, 'Name? Age? Married?' and so on, Herb said confidently that he was 23. The sergeant didn't bat an eye. So far, so good. Herb then had to undertake a medical.

Herb had some real concerns here. He recognised the doctor, a Dr Turner who had served in the Great War and who knew his family well. To his great relief, however, the doctor didn't question his age. He said, through a half-smile, 'You're big enough.'

Herb was passed. However, at this stage, so many other men had felt the need to also 'do their bit', he was told to go home and wait for the call up. In fact, in June alone, 50000 enlisted in the second AIF. Three infantry battalions in South Australia were quickly filled up. These became the basis of the 8th Division.

When he arrived home, Herb realised he should inform his father of his decision and acceptance. With some false bravado, he said, 'I've joined the Army, Dad.'

His father was far from happy or compliant, though. 'I will *not* give you permission to go—you're too young. I won't sign any papers,' he said with strong conviction.

Herb had the final say, though. 'You don't have to, Dad. I'm 23,' he said with a nervous smile, not quite covering an underlying gleam of triumph.

Herb understood his father's reluctance for him to join, but was grateful that eventually he did relent.

Life moved slowly now for Herb as he awaited his call-up.

With some frustration, Herb noticed that in September the Australian War Cabinet created the 9th Division. Maybe it was too late for him. Maybe they had enough men already.

However, in October 1940 he finally received his call-up and, along with his two friends Wally Shane and Bill Pride from Spalding, Herb caught the train to Wayville Barracks, an army training centre in Adelaide. Here, civilian life finished. From now on, Herb was in the Army.

The barracks were set up in the Wayville Showgrounds and the buildings were primitive and draughty, being constructed of unlined galvanised iron. Herb was given a hessian palliasse to be filled with straw as his bed, and was issued with a kit bag and generally ill-fitting army clothes, as well as his dixie and eating utensils. Along with his friends he was placed in a platoon, which was formed into three sections of eleven men each. The section, he was told, was the fighting unit of the army.

Here, Herb met and formed friendships with men from all over South Australia. Among them were Lofty Whaite, a shearer, and Ivan Hanel from Adelaide. Training commenced immediately. Life centred around the 'bull ring', marching, drill, physical exercises, rifle and bayonet practice, and then training with the Lewis gun.

Herb particularly enjoyed the sessions on the rifle range as his years of rabbit shooting had sharpened his eye. He was an excellent marksman, and would nearly always win the overall 'shoot'. Training continued until February 1941. By then, Herb and his platoon friends had moulded into a close unit. Herb had often gone on leave with Bill Pride, and he had also cemented other friendships. They felt they were fit and ready for war. To their concern, however, they had not yet been assigned a battalion as all divisions had now been established. In fact, the 9th Division had been formed and had left for Palestine the previous November.

By early December 1940, the Desert War had begun in the Middle East. Herb had followed each development with keen interest. Mussolini had positioned his Italian Army inside Egypt at Sidi Barrani, ready to attack the British Army who were stationed at Mersa Matruh, about 100 kilometres further along the Mediterranean coast.

Reinforced by the Australian 6th Division, the British Army began the Desert Campaign with a rout that saw the Italians forced back to Tripoli in Libya. By 7 February, the British Army had advanced 800 kilometres and taken 130 000 prisoners, including the major fortresses of Bardia and Tobruk.

The news was welcomed back home; it was a major victory. However, the achievement came at a price as the Italian defeat heralded the entrance of the German Army; this would change the balance of power in the Middle East.

Herb was wondering how this Allied victory would affect him and his chances of going overseas. He need not have worried. In late February, they were told they would be sailing to the Middle East as reinforcements—the first to go.

Herb's training finished with a week of solid finetuning at Woodside, a camp nestled in the Adelaide Hills between Lobethal and Mount Barker. Here, there were training schools, troop manoeuvres, checking of gear and the issue of new equipment.

Finally, in early March 1941, they were ready. Herb entrained from Woodside, along with about 5000 other enthusiastic soldiers, and began the journey to Sydney.

Sydney Harbour was a grand sight. All the prize ships of the world were lying at anchor, ready to form the largest convoy ever to leave Australia. The *Queen Elizabeth*, *Queen Mary*, *Nieu Amsterdam*, *Mauritania*, *Aquitania*, *Ile de France* and others formed an impressive vista. There was much excitement as Herb and some of his Adelaide entourage boarded the

65000-ton express liner *Ile de France*. The mood was contagious. As the grand ladies of the sea paraded in line through the heads of Sydney Harbour, out to the ocean, hundreds of colourful sailing ships, tugs, ferries and moored vessels responded with salutes, horn-blowing, sirens and whistles. So much for secrecy.

Herb Ashby was off to war.

TWO

The Middle East

The sea was a new experience to Herb, as was ship life. The *Ile de France* had been converted from its original role as a luxury liner to fulfil the sparse requirements of a troop ship— space was at a premium. Herb made himself as comfortable as possible in his crowded designated cabin and determined to enjoy the journey.

Initially, as the convoy headed south, the going was pleasurable and reasonably plain sailing. Then, as the great ships turned west around Victoria, directly into the teeth of the chilling winds roaring across the Great Australian Bight, they confronted high and rough seas racing hard against them. The *Ile de France* wasn't equipped with stabilisers and the ship would roll violently sideways while simultaneously rocking up and down, the adverse conditions impacting considerably on the hapless passengers.

Normally, in quiet seas, a meal would demand some patience as four sittings were required in order to feed the large number of incumbents. However, during the Bight crossing, Herb was one of the few who didn't develop seasickness and for five days he virtually had the dining room to himself.

As the convoy drew closer to Fremantle, the seas calmed and Herb would sit at the rail for long periods, mesmerised by the maritime pageant on display before him. Compelled, he would watch as the great ocean liners sliced through the glass surface of the aquamarine sea, creating brilliant straight white lines in their wake. Then, as the lines spread and intermingled, he would marvel as the waves formed beautiful geometric sculptured patterns.

To add to the spectacle, suddenly the *Queen Elizabeth* powered right through the centre of the pack, rushing on ahead. The monarch was the largest liner ever built and had only been launched the previous year—it had been pressed into troop-ship duty even before it could make its maiden tourist voyage. Its top speed was about 40 knots, more than enough to outrun a submarine, and about twice as fast as most of the other ships in the convoy. Herb watched spellbound by the sheer beauty of the spectacle as the ship disappeared towards the horizon.

Some hours later, to Herb's amazement, the *Queen* suddenly reappeared, cruising in from the rear of the convoy. He found out that the ship had simply been on a test run; it had navigated a complete circle out of view of the convoy, and such was its power, had doubled back effortlessly.

Some weeks later, the convoy berthed at Colombo in Ceylon, breaking the journey and allowing the men an opportunity to stretch their sea legs. Herb's first experience with a different culture was peppered with interest and he found the countryside very beautiful, particularly the tea plantations.

Some weeks later, the convoy traversed the Red Sea. Finally, the *Ile de France* anchored at El Kantara on the Suez Canal. For Herb and his friends, this was the end of the line. After negotiating the hordes of Middle Eastern hawkers, a new and often exasperating experience for the Australians, the men boarded a train and headed north over the Sinai Desert, towards Palestine.

Eventually, they moved into Camp Julis, situated on the coastal plain midway between Gaza and Tel Aviv. Herb noted the poor and generally dirty Arab villages dotting the terrain, and contrasted the primitive farming methods with his own comparatively comfortable pastoral experience. He was sure the ancient olive presses, waterwheels and donkey-drawn wooden ploughs had not changed a great deal since biblical times.

By mid-April, a few days after Easter, the military situation changed again. Over the previous weeks the Allies had suffered serious setbacks from their early triumphs. With the Italian forces on their knees, the victorious 6th Division had been sent on an abortive Allied invasion of Greece with disastrous consequences. They were now battling through a heroic withdrawal in the face of a furious German onslaught.

Meanwhile, in February Hitler had agreed to prop up the Italian position in North Africa with a fresh formation called 'Afrika Korps' under Erwin Rommel. Rommel was well known to the Allies as he had commanded the 7th Panzer Division with vigour, throwing the British out of France. He was also known to be a brilliant and hard-hitting commander.

Rommel was already a giant in Germany, and liked to think he possessed the cunning instincts of a fox. Now the legend of the Desert Fox would begin to take shape. His first aim was to recapture the positions lost by the Italians in North Africa. Displaying his mastery of mobile warfare, by 9 April 1941 Rommel had the 9th Division and part of the 7th Division bottled up in the Tobruk fortress in Libya. Accompanying the Australians were elements of the British Army, mainly artillery and armour—Churchill's 'Army of the Nile', as he called it.

Rommel attempted to bypass Tobruk and seized Halfaya Pass, the gateway from Libya to Egypt, but he could go no further—the Afrika Korps came to a sudden stop. Tobruk had to be taken; Rommel could not get around it. His 5th Light Division had achieved a miracle as it was; nevertheless, it was the first Panzer Division ever to be brought to an uncompromising halt. He continued hammering at Tobruk. Further heated battles on Easter Friday, 11 April, precipitated Churchill to proclaim, 'Tobruk is to be held to the death without thought of retirement.'

While Tobruk held, Hitler's timetable for his inevitable attack on Russia was upset. Rommel had to take it. For the Allies, holding Tobruk would not be easy. All their food, ammunition and replacement stores would have to come in by ship under the bombs and guns of the Luftwaffe, which controlled the air space over the fortress.

The 7th Division was about to move to Mersa Matruh fortress on the North Africa coast, about 300 kilometres east of Tobruk, which was now very much the front line. Here they would reinforce and supply the men instituting the gallant defence of Tobruk.

While Herb and his mates discussed among themselves where they might be sent, they were given leave to spend a day wandering around Jerusalem. Herb visited all the traditional biblical sites and could not fail to be impressed by the ancient city. As the centre for three of the great monotheistic religions, Jerusalem is one of the oldest and most holy places on earth, revered by the Jews, Christians and Muslims alike. To walk with devout people of all races seeking to fulfil the human need to believe was a compelling experience.

Herb only stayed a week in Palestine before being transferred by train to Egypt. For a few days he was based at a camp on the Mediterranean coast, Ikingi Maryut, about 30 kilometres outside of Alexandria.

Here, at close quarters, Herb gained his first experience of the grievous price of war. Coming in from the sea, little boats found their way from Greece and Crete laden with injured, sick and often seriously wounded Australian soldiers from the 6th Division, as well as many wounded British soldiers.

Herb witnessed their plight as the exhausted warriors were assisted to medical posts, cleaned up and treated. The soldiers told stories of being overwhelmed by a superior force, including the shock introduction of German paratroopers who secured the airfields allowing German infantry to land. There were many courageous tales of loss and survival during withdrawal.

Herb was then transferred to another staging camp a few kilometres away, El Amiriya, the great army compound outside Alexandria. By now, other stories were coming back about the 9th Division's obstinate and committed stand at Tobruk. It was now becoming obvious to all that Tobruk was developing into a thorn in Rommel's side; he was not just going to be able to run over it and continue to Cairo uncontested. In fact, Rommel rated the port highly, as its possession would shorten his supply line, allowing him to attack Egypt in force. Herb and his mate, Bill Pride (his friend from Spalding, South Australia, who had joined up with him and, in fact, possessed the consecutive number to him), discussed the likelihood of where they would be sent. Tobruk looked to be firming up as favourite.

Of the 23 000 men in fighting units in Tobruk in April 1941, over 14 000 were Australians, about 8000 were British and the rest mainly Indians. The artillery was British, reinforced by 'bush artillery'—Australian infantrymen manning captured Italian guns. The fort was commanded by an Australian, Lieutenant-General Leslie Morshead, who was also commander of the 9th Division. He was renowned as a strict disciplinarian, and was fondly known as 'Ming the Merciless', after the well-known character from the contemporary comic strip *Flash Gordon*. Morshead displayed the necessary strength to stiffen the Allied forces' resolve to stall Rommel.

In early June, Herb, Bill, Lofty Whaite and a large detachment of their Adelaide reinforcement troop—about 100 men—were ordered on board the HMS *Hero*, a small British destroyer.

At last, they were on their way. They knew now their destination would be Libya and that they would be part of what had become known as the siege of Tobruk.

The journey along the Mediterranean coast took about six hours—it was called the Tobruk ferry run. There was some anxiety as the men were aware this route was frequently attacked by enemy fighters and submarines. Their concern wasn't eased as tons of food, ammunition, ack-ack shells, petrol, landmines and acid were lashed to the decks.

Towards midnight, after a thankfully uneventful trip, the ship slowed and entered Tobruk Harbour. The harbour itself was quite small, being a mere 3.5 kilometres long and 1.5 kilometres wide, but it was deep. As the ship navigated towards the wharf, with some relief now, Herb strained to see through the darkness; the harbour presented a sorry sight.

It was virtually a graveyard of ships, some 30 vessels sunk in all attitudes and directions. Some had noses pointing sky-up, some with their masts only above the surface. A few were completely stranded and lying at abandoned angles, the result of magnetic and other mines as well as bombs dropped from planes. It was immediately obvious why the route into the harbour was known as 'Bomb Alley'.

The fortress and surrounding desert were in complete blackness but, in the distance, Herb could hear the whining of air sirens and the far-off sound of bombs clumping. He could also hear artillery fire crashing from within the garrison; the first real sign that he was in a war zone. His heart beat a little faster.

One crash was louder than the rest. 'Hell, that's a big one,' said Herb to a young sailor.

'That's Bardia Bill,' he replied. 'Rommel has a giant 12-inch gun mounted on rails that can hit anything in Tobruk. He'll know we're coming in. The faster we get in and out, the better.'

Tobruk defence lines

The captain of *Hero* was a skilled veteran of this run. Within the hour, he had berthed perfectly in the darkness, discharged his reinforcements and cargo, onloaded his returning passengers and was back out to sea.

Herb and his companions were met on the dock and led a small distance into the garrison where they were ordered to camp on the sand for the night. The next morning, in daylight, Herb was better able to assess his surrounds and was shocked to see the degree of damage incurred on the ancient town.

The port of Tobruk had been fortified by the Italians following Mussolini's occupation in the mid-1930s during the early stages of his empire-building plan. Over a period of five years, the Italians had turned Tobruk into a fortress, constructing massive concrete walls, tank traps and other fortifications. However, when the Allied advance occurred during the previous year, in 1940, the city had been largely destroyed.

The bombing of Tobruk had been severe and the town was now quite devastated; to Herb's eyes it had been reduced to a heap of brick and mortar. Normal life was impossible, the original citizens had left long ago. Beyond was the desert—scrubless plains of sand and sharp, flinty rock, burning white already under what was quickly building to become a blistering sun.

Some trucks appeared and a soldier called to the men, 'You're on the move. You're to join a battalion here. About 40 of you are going to the 2/24th, the rest to the 2/48th. Hop on board.'

To their dismay, Herb and Bill were to be parted. Bill was assigned to the 2/24th, which had recently lost almost a company of men as prisoners, and Herb to the 2/48th. 'Well, I guess Tobruk can't be too big. See you later, Bill.'

They shook hands and Herb climbed onto the tray of a battered truck. Among the other soldiers on the truck were his Spalding friends, Ivan Hanel and Lofty Whaite, also bound for the 2/48th. They stuck together. As the trucks rumbled through the alleyways and streets of the ruined town, negotiating piles of rubble and bomb and artillery craters, Herb tried to orientate himself. They were going west and soon the little convoy moved out of the town.

The Allies had established a strong perimeter around Tobruk from which they had mounted their dogged defence. The outer defensive circle, an approximately 15-kilometre radius around the port, was known as the Red Line, and the inner, secondary defensive circle was called the Blue Line. Within these circles, Australian and British forces fought alongside one another.

The Red Line perimeter included a section known as the Salient, which was hotly contested by both the Germans and the Allies, and was formed when the Germans had earlier launched a three-day attack that penetrated the Tobruk defences halfway between the El Adem Road and the West Coast Road. Here in the Salient, the Germans and Australians were only 200 metres apart. This was where the 2/48th had been sent.

As well as its support units, the 9th Division was basically made up of three infantry brigades, the 20th, 24th and 26th. Each brigade contained three battalions, and the 2/48th was a member of the 26th Brigade, along with her sister battalions 2/23rd and 2/24th, where Bill Pride had been sent.

Herb was pleased to be joining the 2/48th. He knew it was a South Australian battalion, and he smiled as he enjoyed the connection to his old shell-shocked soldier mate from home, the Great War veteran who had befriended him and had been a member of the first 48th Battalion.

The trucks rumbled a short distance out from the centre of the town and harbour, west towards the outer perimeter. Herb noted the dreary, unfriendly landscape. It was little more than a wasteland of rock, limestone ridges and bare brown earth with an occasional wadi and camel thorn bush to break the monotony. The only distinguishing feature was a lone splash of greenery, about 12 kilometres from the harbour. It was an ancient gnarled fig tree, clawing for life, not far from the outer Red Line perimeter. The 2/48th Battalion Headquarters was situated at the fig tree; this was where they were headed.

The 48-kilometre long Red Line followed the original outer defences built by the Italians. These were mainly concrete strong-posts joined by a continuous barbed-wire fence and supported by an anti-tank ditch and minefields. The anti-tank ditches were about a metre deep and 3 metres across. The now incumbent Allied forces had strengthened the wire defences and the minefields.

In fact, Morshead had insisted on extraordinary care and planning to bolster the minefield pattern. New blocks of explosives had been devised to protect the successive defence lines and to provide corridors between them. The posts, or bunkers, which were underground, were well situated for observation, with good fields of fire covering the anti-tank ditch, the minefields and the wire.

The trucks carrying Herb and the other new recruits moved through the second line of defence, the Blue Line, a few kilometres before their eventual destination at the fig tree. The Blue Line was also heavily fortified. Like the outer perimeter, it consisted of a continuous minefield covered by barbed wire and by enfilading fire from platoon-strength bunkers situated approximately 500 metres apart. It also had machine guns and anti-tank guns covering the bunkers and the front. Behind this line was a hard-hitting force of mobile anti-tank guns and tanks ready to be mobilised in the event of a breakthrough.

The trucks finally squealed to a halt some distance from the fig tree. The first thing Herb noticed was the hard ground, strewn with rocks. They were met here by a liaison officer. He pointed, 'That's the 2/48th Headquarters there.' Herb could see nothing—only the sad lone fig tree. The headquarters and associated staff were housed in cement bunkers underground, compliments of the Italian occupation. The regimental aid post was also established here.

'They also print a newsletter from here, *Mud and Blood*. It's written by the 2/23rd men and lets us know what's going on in other spheres of the war, as well as a bit of local news and gossip,' the officer said. 'Mind you, we do have our own local newssheet. It's called *Grubb's Gazette* and reproduces news from the main headquarters newsletter, *Tobruk Truth*.'

'Amazing,' Herb thought out loud, 'you wouldn't know a thing from here.' In fact, they were told, the internal cavity was about 2 metres high and about 15 metres long by 7 metres wide.

The walk to the tree was initially disturbing as they had to be carefully led through a minefield between set tapes. 'You'll get used to it,' the officer smiled. 'Step over the tape though and you're dead.'

The soldier pointed a few metres further west of the tree. 'This area is called the Salient. In May, the Germans tried to break through and we've had nasty tiffs with them ever since. The area I'm pointing to is the outer perimeter, the Red Line. The Hun are only about 80 to 200 yards further on from that. It's "no-man's-land"—but it's ours, we own it.' He said this with conviction and some pride. Indeed, Herb found that the Australians had never lost the initiative in patrolling outside the wire.

Herb was told he was going on to join D, or Don, Company, which was bunkered in right on the front line. To get there, he once again had to negotiate his way through minefields, via taped paths. However, there was an extra complication now. The Germans would often fire random machine-gun blasts across this pathway. As he watched, a machine gun barked from behind the lines, zipping bullets through the sand and spurting dust and dirt skywards around the immediate area. Herb heard the bullets whistle past his head. Gasping deeply, he hit the ground, spraying sand all over himself.

The officer yelled, 'The second they stop firing, get up and run!'

'A man would be mad,' Herb thought.

The firing died away. 'Now!' the officer yelled.

Herb spat the sand out of his mouth and gritted his teeth. He moved quickly into a crouching position, then ran as fast as he could until he reached the relative safety of the outer bunkers and trenches.

'You'll get used to it,' the soldier grinned. 'But you'll have to learn these fixed lines.'

Herb gave a sickly grin, nodded and affirmed he would definitely do that. Herb found that each post was made up of three weapon pits, each about 2 metres deep by a metre wide. They were interconnected by small concrete tunnels which gave access also to underground storage and living quarters. They were designed in a zigzag shape which prevented any bomb blasts from shooting straight along the tunnel.

D Company was comprised of three platoons—16, 17 and 18—each made up of about 30 men. Herb was introduced to the commanding officer of 18 Platoon, Lieutenant Nicky McLellan. They got on well straight away. McLellan came from Bordertown, just up the road from Mount Gambier.

'You'll be with me in 18 Platoon. Welcome. Unfortunately, I've got some bad news for you straight away. I've just heard one of your mates from our area back home who trained with you, Bill Pride, was killed. He trod on a German mine walking into the 2/24th. It was a round one, about the size of a tennis ball with spikes on it. If you step on it, it jumps up to waist height and explodes—does a lot of damage. If it's any consolation, Pride was killed instantly.'

Herb was floored. He had never expected this. He knew the killing part of war wasn't going to be easy, but he hadn't expected it to happen so soon and so violently, and to someone so close to him. It should have been the enemy. The exotic adventure was over. This was serious; one mistake could be fatal. The press at home were calling these men the 'Rats of Tobruk'. He was about to find out why. If he was going to survive he would need to think and act like them, to become one of them.

THREE
Tobruk

It didn't take long for Herb to get his first opportunity to prove himself. Only a few hours, in fact. The platoon commander, Nicky McLellan, introduced him to the men of his platoon. They were dug in at a sector known as Post S23. The 'S' posts (or bunkers) ran from the highest point in the garrison, Hill 209 (Ras el Medauuar), north to the Derna Road and through the steep Wadi Sehel to the sea. 'R' posts ran southeast of Hill 209 in a circle terminating at the Bardia Road, the only bitumen road leading into Tobruk. Hill 209 was vital. It offered the incumbents a tremendous advantage in observation as it towered over most of the ground to the west and north. They always had some idea what the Germans were doing.

Hill 209 had been in Australian hands since 30 April, after a battle known as 'The May Show'. Rommel's storm troopers received such damage at the hands of a gallant 2/24th Battalion that they never attempted another large-scale assault again while at Tobruk.

Post S23, like all the posts, was a little reminiscent of the trenches of the Great War. Besides the cement bunkers and slit trenches, sandbags protruded and protected above the ground.

The first chap Herb was introduced to was a private, Alf Cheney. Cheney was a solid looking man of average height in his early 40s. He was a veteran of the Great War, having served with the Light Horse in Palestine, and had seen it all. He immediately took a liking to Herb, taking him under his wing. Herb was grateful for the show of friendship. He could shoot a rifle and shoot it well, but he was not war-wise. He had received very little combat training and had no experience of patrols or attacks.

Cheney gave Herb a list of instructions. 'First of all,' he said, 'don't be too inquisitive. Put your head up above the sandbags, you'll get it bloody shot off.' Cheney balanced an empty helmet on his rifle butt and lifted it above the parapet. It produced an immediate response from a German machine gunner. Bullets whistled over the top of the fortifications while some clumped into the sandbags, throwing up puffs of dust. Two or three rattled onto the helmet, spinning it around the rifle butt several times. Cheney grinned.

'The Germans are only 50 yards from here and can see everything we do—above the sandbags.' He continued, 'We're fairly well outnumbered, but we manage to maintain no-man's-land as our own. If they step onto it in daylight they are also dead. Right now, Rommel has one German and four Italian divisions out there surrounding us. He's also got one German division in reserve—the 5th Light, their crack division. That means they have about 72500 men. We have about 23000 at this stage— about three to one—of which a third are Australians. So it's pretty fair.' He winked at Herb above a wry smile. 'They had a go at us in April at Medauuar, just south of here,' he said, pointing towards Hill 209, 'but we pushed them back. They also have ten tanks to our one, but they can't get past our fortifications. And they rule the air; they bomb us twice a day, and still we hold them. I reckon we annoy Rommel tremendously,' he said with a satisfied grin. 'The fact is he has underestimated us. He had an insane belief his blitzkrieg tactics would always prevail, and we've stopped him.'

'The second thing I'll tell you is never to volunteer. If you get picked to go, then go—don't argue the point, go and do your job, but never volunteer.' Herb thanked him for the advice and proceeded to meet the other men in the platoon.

By nightfall, he had been placed in a section of eleven men and was settling down for the evening. His section commander, a wiry young corporal, said, 'As soon as it gets dark, we're taking out a patrol. The brass wants us to have a wander in no-man's-land to keep the bastards honest. I need two more with me. Would you like to come?'

Without considering too much, Herb said, 'Too right.'

The corporal said, 'Good. I'll pick you up at this spot at 2200 (10.00 p.m.). It'll be nice and dark then. By keeping control of the area, we deny them information, which gives us a psychological advantage. It also lets them know that we are dangerous,' he added. 'Check your equipment and weapons for rattles. We travel light. Leave your pack and any photos or letters behind—anything that might let Jerry know what unit you're from. We tell the bastards nothing.' The minute the corporal had gone, Herb felt his stomach go tight; a sudden knot wrenched in the depth of his guts. He started to deep-breathe and his hands began to sweat. He fought to control his rising panic, deliberately calming himself. After some moments his breathing settled, then he remembered Cheney's words, 'never volunteer'. Too late.

At 10.00 p.m., the corporal, Herb and a third young soldier crawled out of the bunker and proceeded to cut their way through and under the mass of tangled, coiled barbed wire. After some minutes of this focused action, Herb's stress symptoms settled, allowing him to concentrate on the job at hand. Once they were in the open, the men could crawl more freely, almost slithering over the sandy shale. Very carefully, ever so quietly, they dragged themselves forward on their elbows and thighs. The effort was intense, but after a few moments they were almost at the German lines.

All at once, they could hear talking, the voices resonating in guttural German tones. Herb froze. In the faint light ahead, walking towards them, Herb could make out the form of five German soldiers, obviously on patrol also. They were talking softly to themselves, and were completely oblivious to the small Australian troop. Herb had been told there were no second chances out here; everyone knew the game, and the risks. No warnings were ever given. In a terrible moment he knew he might have to kill a man. His heart thumped.

The corporal signalled to Herb and the other soldier to wait for the patrol to get closer. Herb gripped his .303 rifle, hardly daring to breathe. He drew the rifle butt into his shoulder then took careful aim. This was not a rabbit; it was a human being, but it was also an enemy who would kill him and was threatening his way of life. This was the reason he was here. He aimed at the centre of the approaching third German, a dark apparition now moving towards him. He squeezed the trigger to first pressure, and then held his finger against the firmness, waiting for the signal. The corporal said quietly, 'Now.'

Herb quickly pulled the trigger through the second pressure. The three Australian rifles cracked loudly as one. The sudden noise escaping into the empty desert air shocked Herb as blue smoke and orange flame spurted into the darkness. They were too close to miss. The first three German soldiers immediately reeled, staggered and dropped to the ground, caught in a bizarre dance of death. There was no further movement from them. They were all mortally wounded, the dance over in a second.

The two remaining Germans, shocked by the sudden violence and closeness of the ambush, stammered German expletives into the ether. Realising that their situation was hopeless, they threw their rifles to the ground and quickly raised their hands in surrender.

The corporal yelled, 'Quick, let's get them back. The place will be like a mad house in a few seconds.' He signalled to the prisoners and pointed to the Australian lines. 'Move,' he yelled.

The Germans were also aware that in a few seconds soldiers from both sides would open up, raking the area with bullets. With the two enemy soldiers leading, the five men ran at full pace back to the Red Line. They had no sooner made it to the safety of the trenches when machine guns, rifles and artillery opened up, sending a withering fusillade across no-man's-land and specifically the area they had just been crawling over.

Herb was sitting, catching his breath, relieved to be alive and talking with nervous excitement when his new mate, Cheney, came up to him.

'You mad fool,' he admonished. 'I thought I told you never to volunteer.'

Herb laughed. It felt good to laugh. He knew he'd done well. 'Sorry, but look what I brought back.'

The German prisoners were valuable. They would be questioned at Tobruk then taken back by ship to a prisoner of war camp at Alexandria in Egypt.

Over the next few weeks Herb settled into life at Tobruk. Physically, the conditions were difficult; at times intolerable. By day, the heat was exhausting and at night the temperature could drop to almost freezing, when a cold mist would fall over the battlefield. Herb learned to crouch under his ground sheet when lying in the trench and could often become quite snug. Except for the fleas, flies and dust. The unrelenting dust and sand penetrated every corner and flavoured every mouthful of food.

During waking hours, Herb's time was spent mainly observing the German lines, peering between the sandbags while manning a machine gun—a Bren. It was the first time he'd seen a Bren gun, but he soon mastered its eccentricities, including the tendency for it to stutter forwards with recoil and to shoot high.

Whenever he saw movement, real or imagined, he would give a burst of fire towards the offending sector. It would be answered immediately by a blast of return fire, the bullets thudding into the sandbags. This could happen many times a day—most times with little actual effect, but always potentially dangerous. As such, there wasn't really much opportunity for rest. Even though there could be long indifferent stretches where nothing happened, when on duty he had to remain intently alert.

Every now and then, to break the boredom and fracture the unnerving quiet, an odd kind of shooting match would develop. One aggressor or the other would fire wildly from a far corner of the perimeter and, as usual, the fire would be returned. Then, almost as if by consensus, both sides would steadily circulate the exchange right around the perimeter, moving steadily to the opposite corner, as a Mexican Wave would around a sporting arena. Herb would hear it coming, and when the clatter drew close to his sector, he and his mates would yell, 'Here she comes,' then he would let go a sporadic burst and smile as the gunfire continued along the line.

The only really peaceful period was during meal times. In one of those strange unspoken agreements which sometimes come about in war, both sides observed an unofficial two-hour armistice, beginning at dusk. During this period, neither side opened fire on the other and troops on both sides could emerge safely from their cramped positions. Food, water and ammunition could be brought up and life could be made slightly more bearable. Both armies would break from hostilities, eat their meals, then return to their posts and continue the surveillance and killing. The Germans would signal the end of the armistice by a burst of tracer bullets straight up in the air, and from then on it was business as usual.

In this fashion, each platoon would serve three weeks straight on the Red Line, followed by a week's rest at the Blue Line. While serving on the Red Line, each man would average about two defensive night patrols. The element of deadly surprise meant the patrols were always perilous. During these excursions, Herb regularly confronted the enemy and gradually developed a mental toughness that only experience can bring. He also found that although the Germans were, in general, resolute fighters, they would baulk at the prospect of bayonet fighting; they would surrender rather than run the risk of facing murderous cold steel.

The other duties at night involved food retrieval. As each platoon had three sections, it would be Herb's turn every third night to venture to Company Headquarters to pick up the platoon's food and other necessary supplies on behalf of his section. Great care was taken to walk only between the fixed lines, and if they found a section of the taped pathway had been broken (by bombing, generally) they would repair it.

At the Blue Line, Herb survived in a metre-deep hole he had dug in the shaley ground. Water was always scarce; each man was allowed a half-gallon each day. Fort commander Lieutenant-General Morshead insisted on disciplined routine and meticulous personal hygiene. Each man had to shave daily. This would require sacrificing a little water splashed into a mug, of which some would be used for washing too. The rest was for drinking and cooking. As difficult as life was, Herb soon adapted to this regime and rarely felt thirsty, even though in the desert an untrained person can sweat about two gallons of water a day— four if walking. Some days, the temperature would exceed 50°C, rendering conditions mercilessly uncomfortable. The heat would also make metal guns, containers and utensils virtually untouchable. Flies and fleas continued to create misery in the trenches while dust was a constant problem, complicating breathing and interfering with sight.

To add to this discomfort, every now and then sandstorms (desert *khamsins*) would blow in, often for two or three days at a time, creating misery for the men of both armies. The scorching air, filled with swirling particles of sand, would hit the skin and eyes like razors and reach into clothing, bedding, food and every orifice not kept covered.

The desolate and harsh conditions often got to Herb. However, he realised early on that survival entailed, among other things, sustaining a sense of humour and learning to rely on and to support your mates.

Food supplies were meagre and downright boring, almost solely consisting of bully beef, dog biscuits, tea, milk, sugar and jam. Occasionally, some bread would reach the line, baked locally in Tobruk in simple, wood-fired ovens called 'Aldershot' ovens. Fresh vegetables and meat were rare. Once a camel strayed through the lines, presenting a rare opportunity to supplement the otherwise rigid diet. One of Herb's mates, Harry Dwyer, who came from Bordertown, not far from Mount Gambier, shot it and offered it to the battalion cooks to cut up and serve as fresh steaks. To Herb's dismay, it was tasteless and so tough it couldn't be chewed. The meat was duly sent back to the mess. The next day it was served again as mince, although Herb still couldn't digest it as it was simply too tough.

Even though conditions were harsh, the discomfort was often offset at night by the unique experience of gazing into the black crystalline sky, brilliant with stars. There was a deep beauty in the vision of the moon creeping across the sky, suffusing the rugged desert landscape with an ethereal light. For Herb, there was some comfort in watching the familiar Orion the hunter wheeling above him, still aiming at infinity; a little distorted from here but, nevertheless, a clear reminder of home.

Once, while having a week's rest at the Blue Line, Herb tried to get down to the sea for a swim and a wash, although the relentless dive-bombing prevented him from making it to the beach. German Stuka dive-bombers would saturate targets within the fort, including the beach, at least twice a day. The hated Stukas had a history of shrieking out of the sky in terrifying dives, then dropping 908-kilogram bombs that had screamers attached to them for effect. They had been dubbed 'shrieking vultures' because, with their undercarriages extending like grasping claws from their 'gull' wings, they looked for all the world like vicious birds of prey. As well, the Stuka rear gunners were fitted with powerful and deadly 7.92-mm machine guns which were used to strafe the beach and other locations.

While on his week's rest at the Blue Line, Herb would often meet and befriend men from the other Allied armies. There were Englishmen from the Royal Artillery and the Northumberland Fusiliers, whom Herb found to be good men and brilliant machine gunners. He was intrigued by the names of the units. Whereas Australians were known by a formal number, for instance, the 2/48th, the British were known by traditional names, such as the Sherwood Rangers and the Blackwatch. He also rubbed shoulders with Indians and Poles, who arrived in August. In general, the Poles were dedicated patriots and displayed a great hatred for the Germans; they were absolutely uncompromising and would never take a prisoner. They had vivid memories of the devastation and atrocities inflicted by the invading Germans on their homeland.

Otherwise, there was not much else to do while out of the line—certainly no alcohol, women, parties or entertainment were available. The only opportunity Herb had for alcohol while in Tobruk was as a prelude to one fearful night in early August.

* * *

The battalion had just completed a week's rest at the Blue Line and, on the night of 30 July, had moved back into the Salient to an area called Forbes Mound, relieving the 2/32nd Battalion. The position was a little south of where Herb had originally been stationed, closer to Hill 209, Ras el Medauuar.

It was the middle of the northern summer and the heat was still intense, radiating searing waves across the face of the desert and in its course sapping strength and testing men to the limit. Steel helmets too hot to handle acted like miniature furnaces causing sweat to pour in rivers down dirty, sunburned faces. Gaunt men would sit motionless in their foxholes, conserving energy while peering into the shimmering haze with scorched eyes. After three months in the desert, surviving in stressful and atrocious conditions and existing on a poor diet, general health was beginning to deteriorate. Malnutrition, dysentery and irritating skin conditions were taking their toll on many soldiers. However, morale was high as the defenders of Tobruk were well aware that the longer they held out, the more frustration they would be causing Rommel.

By this stage, both armies had established themselves firmly around the perimeter. Behind Hill 209, the Germans, who held the Salient, had something like 200 Spandau machine guns and about 70 anti-tank guns with strong artillery and mortar support. Regularly, Spandaus would send streams of red tracer bullets across Herb's foxhole, splitting the air with sinister whistling sounds, or otherwise thudding into the sandbags around 18 Platoon's positions. They would be answered by long bursts from the Australian Bren guns, then joined by artillery and mortar fire from both sides until the desert was half obscured in a cloud of dust and smoke.

Because of this murderous fire power and the fact that this tenaciously guarded territory was interlaced with earthworks set

in minefields studded with anti-personnel mines, there were
very few battalion or company attacks from either side.

However, during the early hours of 3 August, C and D
companies of the 2/48th, including Herb's 18 Platoon, were
given ten minutes to be ready to move in attack formation over
the contested open ground. They were to support a frontal
attack by two other battalions, the 2/43rd and 2/28th. Four
platoons of the 2/43rd Battalion were to attack Post R7 in the
south, while the three platoons of D Company of the 2/28th
Battalion were to attack posts S6 and S7 to the north of Hill 209.

The plan was that a success signal, a Verey gun flare, would
be given to indicate that the 2/28th forces had occupied either of
these two posts, then Herb's platoon (and the other five platoons)
were to crawl out of their trenches and move forward in
support. This caused great concern for Herb and his 2/48th
friends. Instantly, he realised that if the two preceding battalions
could not adequately secure their posts, the German machine
guns could effectively wipe out every man moving over no-
man's-land. The Spandaus were always trained on their
positions—'fixed line', it was called—and the minute the 'ding'
started Herb knew their foxholes and bunkers would be
instantly and intensely riddled with fire. It would be almost
impossible to even make it out of their foxholes without being
hit. It would be slaughter. Herb's stomach tightened. He knew
he would go if asked to, but it would not be easy.

This is when they brought out the rum. It was a Great War
tactic, to give the soldiers a bit of Dutch courage before an
attack. The rum was 100 per cent proof and, to Herb, it was
strong stuff. He took a swig. He wasn't that used to rum, or
alcohol generally for that matter, and in the harsh conditions
he felt it burn down his throat to his stomach, then radiate clear
to his toes. The fire then bounced back up again. 'Wow,' he
said, relishing the sudden inner warmth. 'What a kick!' His

inhibitions gone, he made light by standing up and pretending to climb out of his bunker. His grinning mates pulled him back. 'Not yet,' they said. 'Better leave some Germans for us. We haven't got the go-ahead yet.'

The zero hour for the 2/43rd and 2/28th to attack was 3.30 a.m. At five minutes before zero, splitting the silence and heralding the attack, 60 artillery guns opened up a penetrating bombardment, lashing the enemy positions. In return, defensive fire from all arms sprayed over the immediate area that the platoons were due to move over. The moon, which had been three-quarters illuminated, set moments before the Australians were to advance over the inflamed ground; the darkness offering a small advantage to the Australians.

Herb winced at the sound of the massive artillery barrage, the assault setting his ears ringing. He settled nervously back into his foxhole, his Dutch courage all but fled. He strained his eyes through the darkness and tried to identify any troop movements when the scene was momentarily lit up by staccato flashes of the gunfire.

By now, the rum had settled Herb's stomach a little, but it could not eradicate his underlying anxiety. He knew the reality. It would be his turn to enter the killing field the minute the Verey gun signal shot up and flashed in the sky. He fought back thoughts that in a few minutes his brief life could be over. Better not to entertain negativity; concentrate instead on the hope and possibility that the other battalions will win through.

When the bombardment finished, the men from the 2/43rd and 2/28th battalions advanced onto the escarpment leading to their separate targets. Immediately, vicious crossfire from machine guns and mortars slashed them from the front and sides, quickly causing casualties, while invisible 'jumping jack' mines burst from the ground as men trod on them unwittingly.

In the south, the 2/43rd Battalion contingent was quickly

shredded, cut down by the withering broadside. Similarly, in the north, the 2/28th also suffered heavy casualties as it moved through the heavy defensive barrage.

After some time, the men from 2/43rd were forced to withdraw; the fire power was too devastating, their losses too heavy. Four officers leading 139 men left the protection of their bunkers to begin the fight and only 33 men returned unscathed, the four officers either wounded or killed.

Similarly, of the company of men of the 2/28th who began the attack on posts S6 and S7, only a handful eventually reached one of the posts, S7.

The attack on Post S6 failed. The 30-man platoon which began the assault on the post were mown down by bullets, bombs, shells and mines. Only eight men survived the onslaught, some seriously wounded, and they withdrew. This was about 4.00 a.m. At Post S7, a similar fate devastated the two platoons which attacked it. The only four who eventually reached the post had fought a pitched and desperate hand-to-hand battle, killing four of the defending Germans and taking the surrender of six more. The lieutenant-in-command was preparing to signal his success and shoot his Verey gun, but realised that the sack carrying the cartridges had been shot from his back. He immediately dispatched a runner for assistance and waited. An hour or more passed and no word was received from S7; the runner had not made it.

During this period, the fire was so intense as shells burst right around the immediate front that one man from Herb's company was killed and several wounded as they lay waiting in their trenches for the signal to attack.

Herb peered now even more tensely towards the area of the posts, as he and his friends could sense things were not going well. Screams and yells for help echoed back, mingled with sounds of gunfire and explosions. Everybody was waiting in vain for a message of success or failure. Nobody was aware that the runner from S7 had, in fact, been killed. There was no message. It was now about 5.00 a.m., and a few small rays of light were splintering the sky. It would be light by 6.30. Why didn't the signal appear? Herb needed no reminder that it would be sheer carnage if they had to move out in sunlight.

Considering that both attacks had possibly failed, at 5.00 a.m., the 2/28th colonel reported the news to Brigadier Godfrey, the 24th Brigade commander. In his wisdom, Godfrey decided to call off the action. This message was then relayed to 2/48th Battalion commander, Colonel Windeyer. With obvious feelings of relief that his battalion would not need to enter the maelstrom, at 5.15 a.m. Windeyer ordered his waiting platoons be relieved.

However, by 5.20 a.m., the message had not yet reached 18 Platoon. To Herb's horror, a green light suddenly appeared in the sky, unmistakably above S7. It was followed by a red burst, then another green. Fifteen seconds later, Herb's worst suspicions were confirmed; the same succession of lights was fired into the darkness, blazing like a doomsday beacon over the battlefield. It was the signal for success at Post S7. In those few minutes before 5.20 a.m., four reinforcements had arrived at the post and, finding it occupied by 2/28th men, fired the success signal.

Herb gave a resigned smile to his mate. This was not something that could be escaped. Tightening his grip on his rifle, he automatically rechecked his ammunition and steadily moved to join the line of men preparing to do their duty. No one hesitated, even though they all knew there were machine guns trained on them. In the volatile situation, the men were well aware that any perceived movement from their lines would elicit a blistering response from the enemy. They awaited the signal.

A telephone rang, splitting the night and the tension. The

platoon commander, Nicky McLellan, was called to it. After what seemed an eternity, he returned to his men. 'It's off,' he said simply. The relief was palpable. Herb sank to the ground and wished he had some more rum, this time to celebrate. He and his friends had been given a break—his luck had held.

However, for the other battalions, the battle for S7 continued all day. By the end of the following day, there were so many dead and wounded men lying exposed in the midsummer's heat of no-man's-land that the Australians allowed an armistice for the German stretcher-bearers to collect the wounded. At the other posts, the Germans did not allow the Australians similar entitlements.

However, the next day, vehicles from both sides carrying the Geneva emblem were allowed to drive out unmolested into the bare, fire-swept Salient. Wounded and dead from both armies were brought off the field. Amid the vagaries of war, pleasantries were exchanged between the opposing forces.

Unfortunately, the Australian soldiers from the 2/28th who held Post S7 could not be relieved. They were eventually taken prisoner later that night.

On 8 August, five days after the attack had commenced, the 2/48th were pulled out of the Salient and placed in reserve back at the Blue Line. It was now the fifth month of the siege and men were continuing to lose weight and stamina. The dust, heat, vermin, unpalatable food and brackish water as well as continued psychological stress from both boredom and fear, were taking their toll. On 9 August, the battalion was riveted by a driving sandstorm. Conditions were miserable as sand and grit as fine as talcum powder invaded every element of their existence. A few days later, still in reserve, the men had some time to clean their equipment and an opportunity to visit the sea for a swim and a wash. This was Herb's second attempt at entering the ocean, and once again it was foiled. He had no sooner splashed under the waves when marauding Stukas crashed the party. Herb raced for the relative cover of land and decided it was better to be dirty than dead.

At this stage there was talk by the High Command that the Australians might soon be relieved from Tobruk. On 10 August, Lieutenant-General Morshead had, in fact, received plans that the relief would take place during September or October, and that the first formation to be relieved would be the 7th Division battalions of 18th Brigade; they would be heading back to Australia to assist in the defence against the building Japanese threat.

The 2/48th were due to be relieved in October but, of course, the men in the field did not know this yet. Over the rest of August and September, the battalion continued its vigorous and disciplined patrolling duties, as well as rewiring and laying mines. There was rarely a period without incident.

On the evening of 22 August—a night when Herb and his section were designated food retrieval duties—a routine bombing raid on the harbour had developed. That particular evening, there was a great number of ships in the port, triggering attacks by more enemy planes than usual. Parachute flares hung in the sky like great chandeliers, illuminating the desert for kilometres around. The pounding of big guns signalled that an artillery duel was in full force, complete with backing from mortars and the stuttering of machine-gun fire.

Searchlights and red tracers from anti-aircraft guns climbed into the sky, searching for the planes. On top of this, the Germans fired even more ground flares than usual in an attempt to discourage Australian patrols. Vigilance was always required.

Through this confusion and activity, and always aware that they would be visible as dark shadows, Herb and his friends were hauling their rations in a rubber-tyred trailer, generally two pulling and two pushing. As well as carrying ammunition and other supplies, they were dragging a large trough of curried bully beef back to the platoon. Suddenly, without warning, something crashed into the middle of the trough. Fearing it to be a mortar, someone yelled, 'F' Christ's sake, jump!' Immediately the men dropped the trailer and dived for cover, spilling the food onto the desert floor. After some moments, and the realisation that the 'bomb' wasn't going to explode, Herb searched the desert floor and found the projectile to be a burned-out flare. The men looked anxiously at each other, then burst into relieved laughter. The main concern now was how to tell the platoon there would be no dinner that night.

Another almost tragic incident happened a few days later. A message was received from headquarters that an Allied fighter plane would fly in low along Bardia Road and parade over the entrenchments. At this stage, the Germans and Italians had fair command of the air over Tobruk and the men on the ground rarely saw any dogfights or, for that matter, any Allied aircraft. Apparently designed to reassure the men under siege that they were not forgotten, the plane was scheduled to fly low enough to allow the pilot to wave to the men.

Sure enough, in the early afternoon, word quickly circulated that the plane was due across at 3.00 p.m. Right on time, in the distance, Herb could hear the characteristic howl of a fighter plane as it wheeled for its run. He could make out its silhouette against the sky. He expected it might be a Curtiss P-40 Tomahawk, or maybe a Hurricane. The pre-eminent fighter squadron in the Desert Air Force in the Middle East at the time was the Australian No. 3 Squadron, and in June they had been re-equipped with the Tomahawks. It would be great to see one streak across the sky.

At the sound of the motor, men along the intended flight

path—not covered by German guns—jumped out of their foxholes and began waving frantically at the plane, which was now roaring about 6 metres above the ground.

Suddenly, the deadly sound of machine-gun fire shocked the soldiers. Blue flames spat from two 7.9-mm MG-17 machine guns through the propeller arc and from two 20-mm cannons mounted on the wings. Bullets shrieked through the air and smashed into the ground, shattering rocks and spurting dust skywards. This was not a Tomahawk—it was a Messerschmitt Me-109, the lethal German fighter plane.

Wide-eyed soldiers suddenly realised their mistake and ran, diving headlong back into their foxholes. The Me-109 continued on its flight path, sending bursts at any target that presented itself. Herb watched it fly over, almost able to make out the grin on the German pilot's face.

As quickly as it entered the besieged city, the attacker was gone. The Me-109 would not make a second run—the anti-aircraft guns would not allow it.

There was great discussion about the flyover that evening. Just after dark was perhaps the best time of day for the men in the trenches—the 'Rats of Tobruk' as they were nicknamed by the Germans, and were now proud to be called. The men could safely come out of their dugouts and have a yarn. Gossip travelled quickly, as did rumours. How did the plane—and the message—get through? There would be some explaining to do higher up, the men agreed. Luckily, no one was killed, but they'd be on the lookout next time. No official answer was ever forthcoming. While it was good luck this time for the men of the 9th Division, Herb was about to run out of his share.

FOUR

The Salient

On 16 September, the battalion was back in the southern Salient and Herb was entrenched in Post R8. Spirits, generally, were high; there was a grim feeling of satisfaction among the men of Tobruk, knowing that since April they had dragged Rommel to a halt. While Rommel could get no further than Tobruk and the Halfaya Pass, the Allies were allowed precious time to regroup and build up military equipment, particularly American Sherman tanks, plus planes and artillery.

The 18th Brigade had left and was replaced by a Polish brigade. Even though reinforcements were still arriving, there had been a great deal of speculation among the men in the 2/48th Battalion about dates for possible relief, setting off a strong betting spree as to the actual date of departure.

The days were still hot and dusty, and the nights cold. Rommel had not let up his pressure either, with enemy shelling building up to an average of 1000 shells a day, and 'Bardia Bill' and other 155-mm large guns pounding any site they chose to with impunity. It was estimated Rommel had 224 field guns of all sizes, a marked superiority against the garrison's 80 guns. Conditions were just as miserable as they had ever been, but over meal times hopes were always high as rumours of imminent relief flew infectiously around the trenches. In the deep of night, however, from the loneliness of his foxhole, reality weighed heavily on Herb and the rumours seemed just that: rumours. He would listen to the drone of enemy bombers as they circled overhead, searching for a target on which to drop their payload. He would catch the flicker of a searchlight as it probed the sky and momentarily fixed on a plane. Anti-aircraft (ack-ack) fire plastered the sky and somewhere in the precinct there would be a crumping of bombs. In the distance, fighting a private duel, a lone Spandau would chatter and a Bren would snarl back. As the drone of the planes faded, the sound of another squadron of planes would quickly fill the sky. The scenario would be repeated many times during the night. It was never quiet for long.

At this stage, Herb had palled up with another soldier from the Mount Gambier area. His name was Ben Hunt and he had been sent to the battalion for field punishment—he had pinched some fruit out of the food dump and had been caught. Herb had known him before the war, when Hunt had a reputation as a good cricketer. Even though he was considerably older than Herb, they got on well.

On the night of the 16th, the two were selected for duty at a listening post in no-man's-land. Moving forward under the cover of darkness to within 40 metres of the enemy, Herb and Ben settled into a foxhole they had dug for themselves. They had run a phone line out with them and their job was to report any enemy activity. The time passed rather quickly as they both had news from home. The two friends enjoyed each other's company as they swapped stories and savoured the prospect that they might be out of this place soon. It was always good to talk about it.

At the end of their shift, Herb reported on the phone that the enemy was quiet and they were returning to post. Dragging their phone wires with them, the two men started to walk towards their lines, still deep in conversation. However, for a few vital minutes, they had lost concentration, failing to notice that the full moon had been steadily rising and they were now walking directly towards the golden orb. The moon shed its light with cruel brilliance, silhouetting the men as perfectly as ducks in a shooting gallery.

They had just reached the relative safety of the barbed-wire entanglements, where Herb compressed the twisted whorls of metal with his rifle, allowing space to clear it. He had barely jumped the wire when the night was suddenly and violently ripped apart by a burst of concentrated fire spurting from a nearby German Spandau machine-gun nest. The noise reverberated wildly across no-man's-land. To Herb, it sounded like a cannon broadside; it had to be close. Too close.

Before he could react, he was suddenly aware of bullets zipping around his shoulder; he heard them whistling past his ear, some singing as they spiralled off the wire, and some thudding into the desert sand at his feet.

Then, in that terrible instant, a powerful unseen force gripped him and spun him bodily around; picked him up like a giant hand and flung him into the sand on his backside. Within seconds, while desperately trying to catch his breath, he felt a searing pain radiating up his left leg. He knew he had been hit, and was surprised at the heat of the bullet that had torn through his flesh. In shock at the force and his sudden change of fortune, adrenalin and pain caused him to suck in deeply.

He rolled onto his side and grabbed his lower leg. 'I've been hit,' he yelled.

Hunt turned at the sound of Herb's cry and saw his dark form writhing on the ground. 'I'll get you,' he called. 'Where are you hit?'

'I'm okay. I've copped one in the leg. Get away and keep down. There are machine guns everywhere. You'll be hit. I think I can walk. I'm alright,' Herb pleaded.

'No you're not,' Hunt said. 'I'm getting you out of here.'

Herb knew the bullet had gone somewhere through his lower leg, but it was too dark to assess the full damage. It was painful, but he knew he had to try to take some weight on it if he was to get out.

Very carefully, he was relieved to find his limb could take a small amount of weight, enabling him to half crawl, half limp. By now, Hunt had reached him and supported him while he continued to crawl out of the line of fire.

Meanwhile, the other platoon members had heard the machine guns and had seen Herb fall. To them, it looked like he had been badly hit and, instinctively, several men jumped out of their foxholes to help. Herb yelled, 'Get back. Get back, or you'll all be hit.'

One fellow kept coming. It was Norm Leaney. Leaney was from Adelaide and Herb had got to know him well; the two had become good friends. Leaney had a mop of fair hair and was strongly built. He was capable of carrying Herb back.

Herb called, 'Stay there. I'm okay. Go back.'

Eventually, Herb and Hunt crawled up to Leaney, and the three of them half walked, half crawled the remaining distance to the safety of the bunkers.

Here, Herb had a chance to examine his injured leg and establish the extent of his wound. He could see quite clearly that the bullet had entered his leg a few centimetres above the ankle. It looked as if it had almost severed his Achilles tendon.

The platoon commander, Nicky McLennan, said, 'Better get up to the RAP. Looks pretty bad.' The regimental aid post (RAP) was stationed under the fig tree, protected inside the re-inforced underground cave. With the assistance of Hunt and Leaney, Herb carefully manipulated his way through the mine-fields. When he reached the RAP, he was quickly seen by the battalion doctor.

After an initial assessment, the doctor considered he should probably operate on it and wire the tendon together. This, of course, meant Herb's war would be over; he would be sent home.

'No, Doc, I'd rather you didn't. Can I just leave it and hope it heals?' He still wanted another crack at Rommel—but when he was well.

'Well, I'll send you to the hospital at Tobruk and let them decide for you.'

That same evening, he was taken by an ambulance (from the 2/3rd Field Ambulance Brigade) to Tobruk. Tobruk was well served by an efficient medical system so that when a soldier was wounded or taken ill, he was supported by a range of medical facilities along the way until he reached the central 2/4th AGH (Australian General Hospital). The majority of severe surgical cases were able to reach the AGH within six hours. With the lights dimmed, it was a long, miserable, convoluted trip for Herb. The vehicle made several stops at RAPs of other units on the way and, at each unit, Herb would be examined by the local doctor and given a series of injections. He didn't know what they were, but by the time he had reached the hospital he had been given about ten injections. (It was probably a shot of morphine, as one of the chief duties of RAP medical officers was to relieve pain.)

The 2/4th Australian General Hospital in Tobruk, like most of the buildings there, was considerably damaged. Previously the Italian barracks, it was an old colonial-style brick building with attractive arched doorways, situated next to a supply dump. Here, he met two other wounded friends from the Mount Gambier area, Jack Williams and Graham Robinson.

In the morning, Herb noted the shattered windows and the dilapidated state of the building, as well as the devastation of the surrounds.

'Yep,' Williams said. 'Even though there is a large cross painted in the square outside and crosses on the building, we get bombed every day and night. They aim for the supply dump and don't care where the bombs land, although sometimes we reckon they aim for the hospital itself.'

At this stage, there were as many as 600 patients in the hospital. The facility provided top medical and surgical staff and had retained all its specialised departments, including pathology and X-ray. The female nurses had been evacuated two days before the siege began, back in April, and male orderlies had been brilliantly trained to fill their positions. An orderly cared for Herb until he was eventually assessed by the doctor. Herb convinced the doctor not to operate on his leg; instead, he was bandaged firmly and confined to a period of rest.

Herb had just been settled into a bed, when somebody yelled, 'Under the bed. Here they come again!'

Herb had vaguely heard the bombers flying closer, and now became acutely aware of the terrifying shriek as the bombs hurtled earthward. They were directly overhead; the only protection was under the bed. Herb frantically rolled off his bed and waited for the bombs to hit. Within seconds, the terrible shrill ended with massive explosions which detonated right next to the hospital. The concussion pushed in walls and shattered what glass was not already broken. Pieces of metal and timber swished through the air. The hospital became smothered in dust and smoke, and Herb cursed his luck.

Eventually, the dust cleared and Herb climbed back onto his bed. But there was no real respite; within minutes, another squadron filled the sky. This routine persevered for the next two days: on the bed, bombers, under the bed, on the bed, and so on.

Herb quickly learned that bombing was the biggest single factor in the life of the hospital during the siege, creating casualties and continually threatening its effectiveness. He was full of admiration for the staff members. In fact, the bombing was so intense, the staff had created a new word, 'bombsomnia'. No one could sleep. The situation was particularly precarious for men who had been evacuated from the trenches with 'war neurosis', a form of shell shock and stress caused by the general battlefield conditions—'bomb happy' they were called.

On the third day, Herb was grateful to be told he was to be transferred to the 'caves'. This was a staging post for the wounded to either recuperate or to wait for a ship to take them back to Alexandria. There were a number of caves that ran like tunnels under Tobruk, with side caverns leading off and interlacing with each other. The tunnels ended in large caverns, which were well protected and had been furnished by the previous Italian occupants.

This particular one was known as the Docks Hospital and was established in a deep cave under Admiralty House at the docks. It could accommodate up to 100 patients, and had provision for X-ray and theatre. Here, with his friends Williams and Robinson, Herb felt relatively safe, allowing precious time to recover a little.

The three men stayed in the caves until the night of 29 September, when they were transferred to Tobruk Harbour. Orderlies carried Herb by stretcher to a little barge which exited the CCS (Casualty Clearing Station) by a tunnel built by the Italians. The barge moved out into the harbour to rendezvous with a waiting ship, cloaked in darkness. Herb knew he was getting out of Tobruk now. His relief was tempered by feelings of regret at leaving his battalion behind, but he knew they would be following soon. As he was carried by stretcher onto the ship that would take him to safety, his mind filled with images of the mates who would not make it out; the ones who would remain forever here. The price had been high, yet together they had smashed the myth of German invincibility.

Their resilience at Tobruk had tied up Rommel for the summer, forcing him to use one German division and four Italian divisions to hem in Tobruk's one and a half divisions. The Allies had been given time to build up their forces. It was a triumph. And Herb would fight again.

FIVE

Lebanon

It was midnight when Herb was eventually placed on the deck of the English cruiser, the *Jervis Bay*. No talking, no smoking; speed was the essence. Thirty other wounded and sick men embarked with Herb, their stretchers lashed firmly to the deck.

It was cramped, but the sailors knew the drill well. Herb was impressed; even in the dark they were extremely efficient. He was also grateful for the speed. Sporadic gunfire reminded him of the urgency to get away. Every now and then, 'Bardia Bill' would send over a defiant broadside. Within an hour, all cargo had been transferred and the ship cast off. Carefully negotiating the wrecks and other hazards in the harbour, the cruiser then raced for the open sea. It was critical to get as far away from Tobruk as possible before sunrise.

However, it wasn't far enough. As the first rays of morning sunlight sparkled off the Mediterranean, Herb noticed some other glints of light flashing in the sky. He realised, with some anxiety, that a formation of planes was emerging out of the rising sun and fast approaching the ship. Within minutes, his anxiety turned to terror as he realised the planes were the feared Stukas. The silhouette of their characteristic predatorial gull claws betrayed their identity. Herb had nowhere to hide. With motors howling, the planes dived towards the ship.

Strapped to the deck, Herb was indeed helpless. He gasped as the ship suddenly lurched, wrenching violently to one side. What was happening? The instant the Stukas began their dive, the captain had turned the ship so that only the width of the ship was presented as a target, as opposed to the larger surface which would be exposed if the ship was laying lengthwise.

Herb, lying on the deck, was terrified as the Stukas released their load and the bombs emitted their characteristic screaming siren. Herb looked up impotently as the bombs hurtled downwards. They appeared to be aimed directly at him.

Then, to his great relief, he realised the captain's strategy. He watched excitedly as the bombs missed the ship and crashed harmlessly into the ocean, splashing up 10-metre high water spouts. As the planes pulled out of their dive, several continued into a strafing run, raking the side of the ship with their machine guns.

The Stukas had only just retreated when the captain spun the ship violently again. Herb was grateful he was tied down. A wave of torpedo bombers followed the Stukas and lined up for a strike. The ship's bow swung around and pointed towards the planes. Herb marvelled at the captain's skill as the planes roared over the ship, unable to release their torpedoes as the target presented them was too small.

The captain had developed such instinctive timing that he could predict precisely when the torpedoes would be released. As the planes wheeled around for a second run, the captain rotated the ship within that time. His manoeuvring was so effective, not one plane released a torpedo.

Denied their target and with Alexandria not far away, the planes swung from the ship and disappeared into the morning haze now hanging over the desert. To Herb's relief, a few minutes later, under Allied air cover, the cruiser docked at Alexandria at about 6.00 a.m.

From here, Herb was transferred by ambulance to the military hospital where he was prepared for examination. The nurse assisting him was impressed by his deep tan; he had not worn a shirt at Tobruk for three months—virtually the whole time he was there. But on closer inspection the nurse suspected it might be more than a tan at work, adding, 'I am going to wash you. We'll see then.' The truth is, in addition to not wearing a shirt, Herb had not had a decent wash the whole time at Tobruk. After the nurse had given him a thorough scrubbing, he was horrified to realise very little sun had penetrated the ingrained desert sand and dust. He was amazingly white underneath.

By now, Herb's wound had settled a little and he was grateful that when the doctors finally examined him, they decided not to operate. Instead, they placed his foot in plaster.

'We'll give it a few weeks and see how it goes,' said the commanding surgeon. 'It should mend.' That suited Herb.

'We'll send you back up to Palestine to recuperate. If all goes well, you may be able to rejoin your battalion in Tobruk.'

Herb was transferred to Nathanya in Palestine, not far from Haifa. He rested there for a further two weeks at a special rehabilitation unit then, when the plaster came off and the tendon looked to be healing effectively, he was relocated to Gaza, almost ready to return to Tobruk.

By now, it was mid-October. The unit was visited by a Major George Bull, whom Herb knew well. He had been in charge of the 2/48th B Echelon Company at Tobruk. The B Echelon personnel had kept up a ready supply of provisions for the men in the forward posts—food, ammunition, renovated guns and repaired trucks. Major Bull was a veteran of the Great War and had served with the first 48th. He was universally respected and led by example.

From this unit, he picked up Herb and the other men ready for discharge. He told them they wouldn't be going back to

Tobruk as the 2/48th was to be relieved in a few days (23 October). Their job now was to prepare a campsite for them.

With other new reinforcements, the men moved to Camp Julis, the site where Herb had first settled when arriving in the Middle East. Camp Julis was situated on the coastal plain midway between Gaza and Tel Aviv and surrounded by other Australian camps spread over a 35-kilometre region. Over the next few days, the men erected tents for the battalion. Herb was wary, as he killed several extremely poisonous scorpions during this exercise.

When the battalion returned on 25 October, there was much rejoicing. Some soldiers had been under siege for 28 weeks, and the first few days out were spent doing little more than cleaning up and relaxing. Many were sick, all were underweight and most had desert sores. Herb himself had lost a stone at Tobruk and was still recuperating. Julis was a pleasant enough camp. There were poplars and an orange grove, and an adequate supply of good food and Australian beer. There was also a large back-up of home mail and parcels which had accumulated in Palestine, and leave excursions to Haifa, Tel Aviv and Jerusalem were generously granted.

Haifa was only a short bus trip away and was always good for a break. There was a Naafi (Navy Army and Air Force Institute) club there, where drinks could be bought, and the city possessed a fine beach.

As the weeks passed, men began to regain their health. Good food and rest were starting to have a positive effect. It was just as well, as other events in the world were about to impact on them.

News of the Japanese bombing of Pearl Harbor on 7 December brought first shock, then cries of indignation. The Japanese had declared war on the United States and Britain, and, by extension, Australia. The general consensus was that it would be good to have the Yanks in the war; it wasn't going well and every friendly hand would be important. Besides, it wasn't difficult to assess that war in the Pacific could soon threaten Australia, and we would need friends.

This revelation was balanced against some good local news which stiffened the pride of the men of the 9th Division. By late November, the Eighth Army's Operation Crusader was having a considerable impact on Rommel's army. When the British attack opened on 18 November, it achieved total tactical surprise. Armoured brigades, tanks, infantry and the Desert Air Force had combined to muster an intensive and coordinated massed attack against the Axis troops around the Tobruk fortress, making Rommel's situation critical. In early December, Rommel began to pull back to a defensive line at Gazala, west of Tobruk.

On the evening of 9 December, the enemy abandoned their positions around Tobruk and retreated towards Cyrenaica (northern Libya). Tobruk was at last relieved.

They had held out for 242 days—25 days longer than the legendary Mafeking Siege of the Boer War—having resisted everything the Germans could throw at them. What a victory.

By Christmas, most of the battalion were ready to have another crack at the enemy. Christmas Day was memorable in that cyclonic conditions produced drenching rain. Even though mud and slush transformed the normally desert conditions into a quagmire, a meal of turkey and plum pudding plus a bottle of beer kept spirits high.

By mid-January, Herb had regained his normal 12-stone weight and corresponding good health, and considered himself to be 'fighting fit', just in time for the battalion to start active duties again. They were to move north to 'The Lebanon'. Here they were to take over the defensive positions presently occupied by the 6th and 7th divisions. These two divisions were, in turn, to move back to Australia, where news was filtering through that the Japanese had already emerged as a desperate threat in the Pacific.

The Japanese had invaded Malaya and were moving towards Singapore, where they were heavily engaged with the British and the AIF 8th Division. Elsewhere, the Americans were holding out in a vicious siege in the Philippines, at Corregidor and Bataán, against a fanatical and belligerent Japanese Imperial Army.

The concern in the Middle East was that the Germans would try to enter through Turkey and cross the Lebanese–Syrian border. This area was now in Allied hands as the 7th Division, in June 1941 (while the 9th Division were defending Tobruk), had well beaten the Vichy French in a surprisingly bitter and costly campaign. The other concern was that the Germans would attempt to land on the nearby coast, so the battalion was also to be used in coastal defence.

The trip north was interesting to Herb. The battalion left Haifa on 18 January by motor convoy and passed through incredibly beautiful scenery. The modern road wound through tunnels and cliffs, with the blue Mediterranean on one side and soaring, rugged cliffs on the other, often racing up to wooded and snow-topped mountains.

They passed through groves of oranges, mulberries and olives, and towns as old as history itself. At Acre, monuments to the crusaders and Richard the Lion-Heart still stood. At Tyre, where the convoy had a rest, the history reverberated back five millennia to the ancient Phoenicians (the first large-scale Mediterranean traders) who had lived in this area.

Just before Beirut, the capital of Lebanon, they crossed the Nahr el Kelb, or Dog River. Here were details of the conquerors who had engraved their names on the rock face over centuries, beginning with the great Egyptian, Ramses II, in 1298 BC. Some of the inscriptions of the previous nineteen invading armies had been chiselled into the rock itself, and were in various states of deterioration. Later ones were recorded on plaques cemented into the cliffs, including one for the first AIF Light Horsemen who passed this way on their 'Great Ride' to Damascus. There was also one for the second AIF 7th Division from the previous year.

Herb, barely twenty years old, and thrust into a violent global conflict in one of the most exotic regions of the world, could not help but be interested in history; he was now part of it. The convoy continued through Beirut then further north, past the ancient Byzantine city of Byblos, where Herb learned the alphabet was created, and from where the Bible is said to have derived its name.

Eventually, on 19 January 1942, the battalion drove through the old crusader port city of Tripoli and, just beyond, they pulled up at Le Gault Barracks, their final destination. The old French barracks were roomy, able to accommodate the entire battalion. Here they were to commence hard training and spend time patrolling the border: garrison duty, it was called.

At this stage, Herb was approached by the platoon commander of 17 Platoon, Lieutenant Jim Waring-Smith. Herb had great respect for Jim Smith. He knew him to be a financier in a bank before the war and considered him to be a good man. At 6 feet tall, fair in complexion and very fit looking, Jim was an intelligent leader and treated his platoon well. 'How would you like to come over? I need a good section leader. Would you take rank as a corporal?'

Herb replied, 'Yes, I would be pleased to come over. But I don't want to become a bloody "Jack" [corporal].' Herb did not believe that he was ready for the role of leadership at this stage. The paperwork didn't take long and within a couple of days Herb found himself in 4 Section, 17 Platoon.

It wasn't a difficult decision for Herb to change platoons as some of his friends who came in as reinforcements with him were already in 17 Platoon—Ivan Hanel, Wally Shane and Lofty Whaite. Hanel was in 6 Section and he introduced Herb around. One person he met and liked was Stan Gurney, who had arrived at Tobruk at the same time as Herb. Gurney was older than most—in his 30s—and was an easygoing, likable chap. He was solidly built and just under 6 foot.

On 28 January, the battalion welcomed their new commanding officer, 35-year-old Lieutenant-Colonel HH Hammer. Hammer was known to be tough and reports circulated that he had been in the thick of the skirmishing during the Greek campaign with the 16th Brigade. He called for a full battalion parade next day and informed the unit that his motto was 'Hard as Nails'.

In the days that followed, it wasn't difficult to see how he gained his sobriquet, 'Tack'. He hammered, the battalion responded, yielding like nails to his command. The men of the battalion were keen to be battle-fit again, particularly when they heard the news that Singapore had fallen to the Japanese on 15 February. Perhaps they would be sent home like the 6th and 7th divisions.

However, the battalion stayed at Tripoli until 22 April, when they moved into tented camps 14 kilometres southwest of the town, among olive groves around Bechmezzine. This camp was more suited to hard training as they often went on three-day 'live out and train' exercises over the rugged countryside. Their time was spent between frustration at not being able to get back to Australia and utter exhaustion at the hard mountain walks in full battle gear.

But there were rewards. One leave period allowed Herb to visit the fabled cedars of Lebanon. There was a grove of about 400 trees, heavy with snow, some of them thought to be at least 1500 years old. Once used extensively throughout the ancient and modern worlds (even some of Australia's early stately homes were built from these cedars), these were now some of the few remaining.

Another highlight was a visit to Baalbek down in the Bekaa Valley, not far from the Syrian border. Standing on a huge acropolis were six massive columns—the Temple of Jupiter. Seventy feet tall, the columns were the highest ever erected. Indeed, the ruined city was known to be one of the great sites of antiquity.

Another day, Herb crossed the border into Syria and visited one of the most notable classical crusader castles still standing— the Crac des Chevaliers, the 'fortress of the knights'. It stands near the road running between Aleppo and Damascus, and in medieval times, anyone who controlled this area controlled inland Syria.

Herb was once stationed on a two-week platoon patrol in the mountains overlooking the ocean. Despite the fact that their main task was to scan the horizon to ensure no enemy landed by sea, the wild beauty of the countryside was often lost to him as he and his fellow troops were regularly exhausted after enduring muscle-screaming climbs around the region.

The platoon had to provide their own food for the duration of the patrol and towards the end Herb became concerned as their carefully planned supply of rations began to run short. He soon realised why. Herb had noticed an attractive Lebanese woman approaching the platoon at about the same time every day. He later found out she was a prostitute, bartering her favours for a tin of bully beef.

Towards the end of June, Herb was allowed some leave to visit Beirut. He enjoyed the strong French influence, the sidewalk cafes and beach settings. It was also interesting to experience the cultural balancing act between the Christian and Muslim communities. For centuries they had survived together harmoniously, yet the balance of power had been dramatically unsettled following the unfair pact set up by the European victors of the Great War. There had been troubles ever since.

Herb had returned to Tripoli for a few days and was loading artillery ammunition on ships bound for Tobruk when he received word that the fortunes of his local war had changed again dramatically. Rommel had been attacking hard at Tobruk and, at the same time, the Eighth Army had been severely mauled at a fortification dubbed Knightsbridge by the British soldiers.

Earlier, when Rommel had been pushed back to Gazala the previous December at the end of the siege, British Eighth Army strategists had ordered their units to build a fortified chain of defences dotted over what could have been, if joined up, a unified and strong front line stretching from Gazala to Bir Hacheim—the Gazala Line. Knightsbridge was one of these six strongholds, and was about 150 kilometres south of Tobruk. Along with Bir Hacheim, Knightsbridge helped prevent Rommel from forcing his way around this flank. The battle here was to earn the name the 'Battle of the Cauldron' because of the seething land and air battles fought in the region.

Herb received the chilling news, 'You can stop loading, men. The Gazala Line has gone. Tobruk fell a couple of days ago on the 21st. The ships won't be sailing.' The news shocked Herb—as it did every man who had laboured and bled at Tobruk, for so long and at so great a cost. How could this happen? Thirty-five thousand troops had been made prisoner and an enormous amount of equipment, food and ammunition—2000 vehicles, including 30 tanks and 400 guns, and enough fuel to commence Rommel's drive to Cairo—had fallen into German hands in a single day.

The news hit all the Allies hard, including Churchill, who considered the loss to be a disgrace. He and the free world still badly needed a convincing victory against the Germans and, politically, Churchill was now in danger. Rommel fared better with Hitler, who gleefully rewarded him with a promotion to field marshal the next day.

By 25 June, the Eighth Army had withdrawn to Mersa Matruh, about 230 kilometres inside the Egyptian border and about 120 kilometres from El Alamein Station. Rommel was quick to follow and now appeared rampant, intent on fulfilling his prediction of making Cairo in ten days.

That same night, Herb went to bed indignant that others had lost so quickly what he and his friends had fought so long to hold. At this stage, every man in the 9th Division still had dreams and expectations of going home, yet most would have been keen to stay here and seek revenge on the local enemy, given a chance. They didn't know it, but they didn't have to wait long to get that chance.

Herb and the men of the 2/48th were woken that same evening at midnight. They were ordered to pack their gear and to get themselves onto waiting trucks. They were told they were to be put on a war footing, so all colour patches and badges were to be concealed, digger (felt) hats were to be replaced by steel helmets and all distinguishing features on their vehicles were to be obliterated. No one must know who they were or where they were going.

The higher ranking officers had been told their destination was to be a close-guarded secret. They would travel east first to let the men (and others) think they may be headed to the Syrian Desert for training and probably home, but then they were to turn south for Egypt—to El Alamein.

As they didn't have enough truck drivers at such short notice, the platoon members were asked if anyone among them could drive. Herb had driven trucks before the war, so he put his hand up. That way, at least, he'd get a front seat. It was a brand new six-cylinder Ford, a three-tonner, made in Canada. It was dual wheeled and only two-wheel drive, which Herb anticipated could be problematic with the sand terrain, but it drove well. There was no canopy, and his contingent of twenty men (two trucks to a platoon) simply sat on their kit bags in the back, which was a plain flat tray and rather uncomfortable, while Herb and the other driver shared the front seat.

Herb's companion driver was from the transport pool and was in charge. They got on well, even when he asked Herb, 'Where did you drive?'

'Out in the paddocks, super-spreading,' he replied, referring to his time on the farm spreading 'super phosphate', a fertiliser.

The driver smiled. It wasn't a problem.

In the early hours of 26 June, Herb's truck was one of the leaders of a very long convoy pulling out of Tripoli. It was spring and cool, and the men were bemused as they headed into the hills behind the city, driving almost due east. As the sun rose, the mountainous tracks widened into a panoramic plain. Just before they reached Homs, the lead truck rendezvoused with a waiting British provost officer on a motorcycle, who then lead the convoy south. So, thought Herb, we aren't going to train in the Syrian Desert. We are either going home or off to fight Rommel.

The convoy, which Herb realised now consisted of most of the 26th Brigade and was a massive 90 kilometres long, had its first break at Baalbek for breakfast. The morning sun caught the six remaining pillars of the Temple of Jupiter, which never ceased to impress.

The convoy pulled out at 8.00 a.m., and Herb and his co-driver drove all that day and through the night until they reached the Sea of Galilee at about 5.00 in the morning. Here, they boiled a cup of tea with water from the lake and had some breakfast. They also took a quick swim as they weren't sure when the next chance to bathe might avail.

At 6.30 a.m., they were on the move again. Just past Tiberias, Herb's truck moved into the lead position and some hours later, when they were approaching Jerusalem, Herb accidentally took a wrong turn. As they drove through the ancient city streets, the men in the back tray of Herb's truck began to sense they were in the wrong place. 'Hey Herb. This place looks good enough. Why don't we stay here?'

The humour was a little lost to Herb as he looked back on hundreds of trucks in his rear-vision mirror snaking their way behind him—each one obviously also realising this was not right. Eventually, two motorcycle policemen caught up to Herb. Barely smiling, they redirected Herb out of the city, much to the amusement of his platoon friends and, indeed, the ensuing column. Outside Jerusalem, the convoy stopped for refuelling. Petrol was three pence a gallon, and it was a memorable sight to see well over 50 trucks lining up at a local petrol station.

Further south, the convoy passed through Beersheba. In this arid desert region, 27 years earlier, the Australian Light Horsemen had covered themselves in glory. Herb could imagine the 800 Light Horsemen heroically sprinting over the open plain, racing into thousands of Turkish guns in one of the last great cavalry charges in history.

They were now in the Negev, which was part of the Sinai Desert and extended south from Beersheba and east to the Dead Sea. The road south over the Sinai was made after the Great War by simply laying tar over the sand and it was still very serviceable. They travelled about 300 kilometres that day and camped at dusk just before the Suez Canal.

It was the first time that two of the 9th Division brigades— the 24th and 26th—had bivouacked together on this journey. With 50 trucks to a battalion in an entourage encompassing six battalions and all their support units, there were literally trucks everywhere—hundreds of them and thousands of men.

And there was energy. Here the battalions were told of their final destination. They would not be going home—instead they would be continuing to the Western Desert—to fight Rommel. The reaction was one of mixed emotions. The disappointment of not going home was tempered by the excitement of a reckoning with the Afrika Korps. All the vehicles were refuelled and strict blackout precautions imposed. Everywhere there were RAF units with their bombers parked on desert landing strips. During the night, Herb could hear planes taking off on missions or returning from them. The war was still very much active, and close, and he realised now he was soon going to be a part of it again.

At daybreak next morning, 30 June, the convoy crossed the canal into Egypt on a swaying vehicle pontoon. By now, the men had accepted the change in destiny and were busting for a fight. They had just heard that Rommel had pushed the Eighth Army out of Mersa Matruh and his army was marching towards Cairo. The Brits were in flight, and Rommel was in blitzkrieg mode again. The only defences stopping him were the partly prepared positions at El Alamein. Here, the remaining British troops had dug in and were wiring and laying mines, while past them poured the transport of their retreating army.

Herb noticed the convoy was moving at an eager, cracking pace as it drove along the foul-smelling but euphemistically named Sweetwater Canal Road towards Cairo, slowing perceptibly as the vehicles negotiated head to tail through the city itself.

They stopped at Mena Camp that early afternoon for a meal and for refuelling. Herb noticed they were not far from the famed pyramids and the Sphinx, which in turn appeared passively unimpressed at their presence; they'd seen invading armies before—many of them.

From here, they received orders to be at El Amiriya by dawn next day to be ready to fight. Herb knew El Amiriya—it was the great army compound about 30 kilometres outside of Alexandria where he had been based before being shipped off to Tobruk. He pulled his truck out of Cairo at about 9.00 that evening and headed north towards Alexandria. It was difficult driving as the convoy had to move without lights. There was a little moonlight early on and the road itself was reasonable—a narrow strip of bitumen set in a sea of sand—but later the moon dropped out of sight and Herb could barely make out the colour of the sand from the road.

Each side of the 160 kilometres of road from Mena to El Amiriya was a continuous line of traffic. Heading towards Cairo, often two lanes deep, were various units of the retreating Eighth Army, ordinance vehicles, armoured cars, artillery of all sizes and truckloads of exhausted troops, personnel and tanks. The only vehicles moving towards El Amiriya were those of the 9th Division, which crawled along, sometimes at a snail's pace, sometimes gridlocked for hours.

Finally, Herb pulled into El Amiriya in the early hours of the next morning. It had been a herculean undertaking for all the drivers, negotiating 1600 kilometres with virtually no rest, intently watching the road day and night. Herb was grateful to finally leave the truck behind. He badly needed sleep; he knew he would be in action soon.

PART II

Little El Alamein

SIX

Shammama

While the Australians enthusiastically prepared defensive positions at El Amiriya, they were not aware that further west in the desert, this day, 1 July, was arguably to be one of the most critical of the whole campaign. Even though Rommel's troops were exhausted, he gambled on a desperate push to create a breakthrough. He struck with all his might against the remnants of the Eighth Army, who were spread along what is now known as the El Alamein Line. The intended breakthrough by the 21st Panzer Division and the 90th Light Division caused the desert to erupt with all the drama of epic battle. Rommel was confident he would be on the outskirts of Alexandria by nightfall.

Great clouds of dust billowed from the battle site, accompanied by the low throb of artillery and cannon fire; the signs clearly observed 80 kilometres away at El Amiriya.

'Boy, there's some "blue" going on out there,' one of Herb's mates commented. 'I hope they can hold them till we get there.'

In the meantime, Herb's platoon mates had stumbled on an unexpected bonus while they were waiting for orders and the outcome of the battle. They had found a truck loaded with 9 per cent proof Canadian beer which the retreating Brits had 'saved' from the Naafi canteen at El Amiriya. In their haste to get to Cairo, the truck was left behind.

'Keep this quiet,' the call went out. Over the next few days, the beer generated great moments of joy for the platoon.

Back at El Alamein, the Eighth Army commander, General Auchinleck, over the same few days had outplayed Rommel and fought him to a standstill. There would be no breakthrough. But the battle was costly to both sides. Auchinleck needed reserves and time to consolidate. Rommel certainly needed time also. Both armies had lost many men, tanks and artillery.

On 3 July, the commander of the 2/48th Battalion, Lieutenant-Colonel 'Tack' Hammer, received the orders he was waiting for. Along with other units, he was to move to the front line as reserve for the Eighth Army. Two battalions of the 24th Brigade, the 2/43rd and 2/32nd, left on 4 July, and, in the early morning of 6 July, two battalions of the 26th Brigade, the 2/48th followed by the 2/24th, began their move to the El Alamein Line.

Once again, as part of a long motor convoy, Herb settled into a truck—this time in the back—for the 65-kilometre haul west to their intended campsite at Shammama Halt, about 15 kilometres east of El Alamein. The splendid tarmac road hugged the coast and was accompanied by the ever-present railway line and telephone posts snaking alongside it. On this trip along the Mediterranean, with his bottle of Canadian beer in hand, Herb had more chance to appreciate the myriad hues of green, blue and turquoise, and to notice the palms as they reared from the white sands.

When they arrived at Shammama Halt, they found that the other battalions from the 24th Brigade had been moved from here, their original site, and had dug in a little further south at Ruweisat Ridge.

Shammama was about a kilometre from the coast with the railway line further south. The men of 17 Platoon were delegated positions and quickly dug in, ready for anything. They had just finished drinking the last bottles of their precious beer

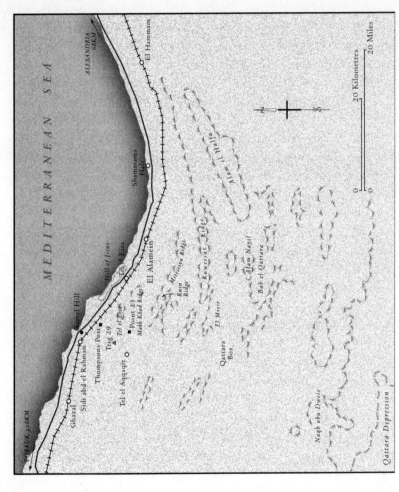

El Alamein

when they heard a squadron of planes approaching. They were not too concerned. Conditions in the air had changed tremendously since Tobruk days and the men were already used to hearing mainly their own Desert Air Force planes fly overhead.

These planes were at about 15 000 feet, and one man idly put his beer down and stood up to look. 'Nah! They're ours,' he drawled disinterestedly. 'Keep digging.' Then, suddenly, Herb heard an ominous whistling sound. He looked up, horrified. There were sixteen bombs hurtling down towards their campsite.

'Jump!' he yelled. 'They're Jerry's.' Herb sprawled onto the floor of his newly made gun pit and covered his head as the bombs exploded within the vicinity of D Company, several landing around 17 Platoon. When the dust settled, he heard that a gunner had been killed from a nearby anti-tank regiment and five men were wounded from his D Company, including Norm Leaney, the friend who helped him when he was wounded at Tobruk. He had been ripped apart by shrapnel and was quickly evacuated to the RAP.

While Herb was trying to ascertain the seriousness of Leaney's wounds, the air above suddenly burst into life again. Herb looked up. A German Messerschmitt and an RAF Spitfire were engaged in a deadly skirmish. The two planes roared across the Shammama Halt airspace about 30 metres above Herb's head, the Spitfire chasing the Me-109 round and round at a dizzying speed.

Then, suddenly, as the Me-109 straightened after one turn, the Spitfire pilot grabbed an advantage. He pressed his trigger and poured a few seconds' burst of cannon fire at the Me-109. The rounds slammed into the German plane's left wing, cutting the metal like a knife. The plane shuddered and jerked violently upward as a piece of the wing spun off and whipped into the slipstream. The Me-109 was low enough to be shot at from the ground, but Herb and his friends resisted. This would prevent the Spitfire pilot from claiming a 'kill'. It looked just to be a matter of time anyway as the RAF pilot was forcing the Me-109 lower and closer to the ground. The men on the ground yelled encouragement to the Brit, 'Bring the Hun down.'

Then, in a blur of speed, diving in from behind the morning sun, another Messerschmitt whirled in to attack the Spitfire. The Spitfire pilot had been completely surprised. It appeared he had little choice but to break off his attack for his own protection.

The pilot pulled back on the joystick, reeling the plane upwards to escape the predator. Within a few seconds, all three planes had vanished. The British pilot had opted for retreat as the better part of valour, but had left one Messerschmitt limping from the battlefield, dragging a wounded wing. Herb noted again how the fortunes of war change so quickly.

Over the next few days, the men were treated to many dogfights as the pace of the conflict escalated; it would not be long before the Australians would be called to action as well. Indeed, at midday on 8 July, the 2/48th were given orders to undertake a night attack two days later. As part of Auchinleck's plan to switch the play to the northern section of the El Alamein Line, the 26th Brigade were to seize various important features. (Up until now, over the last week, most of the action had been in the southern and middle sectors, mainly by the New Zealanders, Indians and South Africans.)

The 2/48th objectives were to seize the Hill of Jesus (known as points 26, 23 and 33, the numbers relating to the height in feet above sea level) and then to take the Tel el Eisa Railway Station (the southern part of points 23 and 26). 17 Platoon received their instructions on the evening of 9 July, Lieutenant Smith passing on the plan. 'We will be attacking first light tomorrow morning. A and D companies are to capture the coastal ridge, particularly the Hill of Jesus first. It's almost 10 kilometres west of El Alamein, past the South Africans' area. It is important we take it as it will deny the enemy observation of the Eighth Army's forward lines.'

'The Hill of Jesus?' someone asked.

'Yes, apparently Jesus gave a sermon there 2000 years ago. The Padre doubts it, I might say. Long memories in the Holy Land. Once we take this hill, we [D Company] then combine with C Company and swing left to capture the Tel el Eisa Station. Then we hold there. In the meantime, the 2/24th Battalion will move along the coast to our right and capture point 33 and then the Tel el Eisa feature itself [*tel* is a hill], south of the railway line.'

That evening, Herb took his place in the convoy that left Shammama Halt and quietly contemplated the coming battle. As usual, his stomach was knotted with anxiety as the trucks drove the 35 kilometres to the start line. By midnight, all men were in position, ready to move through the minefield.

By 1.30 a.m. on 10 July, the whole battalion had moved through the wire and formed up, still in perfect silence, ready for the attack phase. C and B companies led off and stealthily advanced towards Point 26.

They encountered very little resistance: the 25 Italian soldiers from the Sabratha Division who were maintaining that position were caught still sleeping and by 5.00 a.m., all had surrendered. The Italian colonel, attired in brightly coloured pyjamas, protested loudly at being awakened so early.

After the capture, Herb's D Company together with A Company moved through this position to take their objectives— Point 23, about 2 kilometres further on. Would they be as lucky? Herb's stomach was settling a little now as the first fingers of dawn spread over the desert. Action was imminent. There was no talking or smoking.

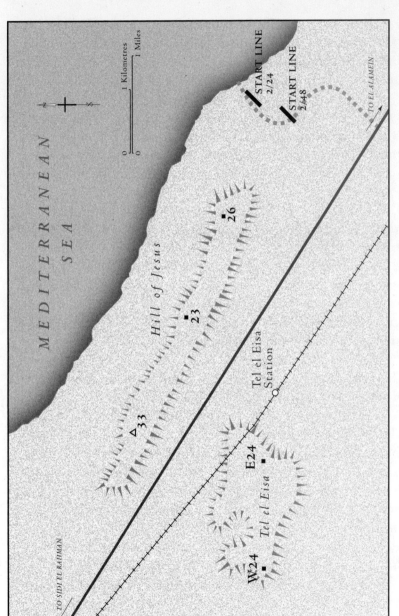

Tel el Eisa Station

Then, in an instant, the enemy alarm was raised. They had been spotted. The two companies were immediately riddled by intense fire from both rifles and machine guns. Herb went to ground, cursing, bullets whizzing overhead in the eerie half-light.

At the same time, over to the right, the 2/24th Battalion was preparing to take Point 33, the dominant ridge of the coastal strip—a position which gave the enemy observation over kilometres of the Allies' El Alamein defences. They were waiting for a success signal from A and D companies for their attack on Point 23.

Then, from behind Allied lines, the Italian resistance was answered by the largest cannon barrage the Middle East had yet seen. An almighty crash thundered and reverberated through the air; flashes sparkled as cannons discharged along the line, searing the darkness. Gunners from British and Australian artillery regiments pounded points 23 and 33 with unrelenting gunfire. Barking 25-pounders created large clouds of dust and smoke as darts of burnt cordite spat from their barrels.

The noise was ear-splitting—enough to wake the dead, Herb thought. He winced, waiting for the air to clear, grateful that he wasn't on the receiving end of the bombardment.

The moment the artillery assault ceased and the smoke cleared, both companies were ordered to crawl towards Point 23. Now, it's on. Herb methodically inched towards the enemy, oblivious to the sand and dirt grinding at his elbows, intent only on the enemy and the job ahead. A few metres out from the still-stunned enemy lines, the Australians stood up on signal and charged as one. Herb, together with the other 200 men from the six Australian platoons, legs working like pistons, screamed at the top of his voice as he ran. It felt good to release the tension.

The effect on the Italians was demoralising. They were expecting tired South Africans, not fresh, fit and keen Australians. For a moment, the Italians rallied. Gunfire rattled between the men from both armies. Herb didn't hold back. He fired with deadly aim, clinked the spent shell out, reloaded and fired continually as he ran.

Men fell in the early morning darkness. Within minutes, right along the line, Italian machine-gun posts were destroyed and gun pits devastated, fierce hand-to-hand confrontations shocking the enemy into submission.

Realising the situation was hopeless, Italians began to appear, like ghosts. They emerged out of the smoke of battle, in the sepia and purple of the early morning, waving anything white— underpants more often than not. It was almost comical to the men of the 2/48th, as they lined up the stunned Italians. There were hundreds of them. Two Australians, one on either side, armed with a Bren gun each, marched the prisoners back to the Australian positions and the POW encampment. If any Italian stepped out of line, a smart burst from the Bren sprayed across their path quickly straightened them out.

With Point 23 in Allied hands, the 2/24th Battalion commenced their attack on Point 33. By now, the Afrika Korps had well and truly regrouped and the area came under heavy enemy anti-tank, mortar and machine-gun fire. Herb could hear the commotion clearly as he was lining up for the next phase of the plan, the swing down the Hill of Jesus to attack Tel el Eisa Station.

At 7.15 a.m., C Company and D Company advanced towards the station area. Suddenly, the enemy fire switched from Point 33 to Herb's advancing troop. The whole area from the railway line to the sea—a 4-kilometre distance—was alive with flame, smoke and vicious crossfire from German and Italian machine guns. Herb quickly dug in, cursing the hard ground. To add to the noise and confusion, the air war started again in the skies above. Dogfights blistered the air space.

Then, once again, on signal the two companies, C and D, rallied to charge the enemy's positions at Tel el Eisa Station. All chance of surprise now lost, the men of the 2/48th encountered stiffer resistance this time. Much hand-to-hand fighting followed with hand grenades and Bren guns creating a great deal of damage. Firing as he ran, Herb raced into the thick of the melee, men falling from his deadly aim.

The skirmish, though fierce, was over reasonably quickly. The enemy were overpowered, white flags of surrender appearing over the battlefield. One of Herb's mates from 17 Platoon, Paddy Malone, noticing a white flag flapping not far from his position, moved swiftly but warily towards the flag.

A few moments later, Herb caught sight of Malone, beaming widely and walking behind about 100 dishevelled Italians. One of the prisoners was carrying Malone's rifle for him. Malone called out cheekily to platoon commander Jim Smith, 'G'day, Lieutenant. I've captured one hundred of the blighters. I want a VC [Victoria Cross] for this.'

Smith laughed. 'No, you've got to bring in 1000 before you'll get that.'

The humour momentarily eased the tension, although not for long. The air war above them was still being fought non-stop at a voracious pace. It was now about a quarter to ten and 40 Stukas were circling above looking for a target. Battalion Headquarters was situated on the reverse slopes of the just won Point 26, and suddenly Herb was aware of the hideous whining characteristic of the attacking Stukas, as the bombs screeched through the sky towards them.

Dust and smoke once again consumed the immediate area and Herb winced from the concussion caused by the exploding bombs. However, Herb's attention was elsewhere, in another corner of the sky, as he became aware of the sound of roaring motors racing towards him. Emerging through the now patchy smoke, almost in a blur, he caught sight of two planes fixed in a death wrangle.

An RAF Spitfire was in hot pursuit of a Messerschmitt 109. The Spitfire had gained the upper hand, forcing the Me-109 dangerously low until they were both zipping along about 10 metres above the desert floor. The distance between the two planes narrowed and Herb heard the familiar stuttering of machine-gun bullets blazing from the Spitfire.

The bullets poured into the wing of the Me-109, some hitting the fuselage. Abruptly, a splash of flame burst through the wing, turning the Me-109 into a virtual flamethrower in a matter of seconds. There would be no escape for this plane. Brilliant fire streamed into the wind from along the fuselage. The plane twisted wildly, then dived towards the desert. In a terrifying moment, Herb thought the plane was going to crash directly into him.

Herb stood, transfixed, primal fear compelling him not to move. At the last second, the plane twisted and careered past him, discharging a trail of blue smoke fanned by the slipstream. With the gut-wrenching sound of crumpling metal, the plane crash-landed some 10 metres from him. There was no chance for the pilot to escape. A parching cloud of dust swirled around the plane as it continued to grind into the shale.

The Spitfire pilot roared past his downed enemy, metres away from Herb. Pleased with his kill, he performed a victory roll to the cheers of the soldiers on the ground and quickly disappeared from the scene.

Herb snapped out of his momentary shock and raced over to the crashed Me-109. The plane was smouldering and had ripped a large gash in the earth. The pilot was obviously dead. He would have to be dug out; there was nothing Herb could do.

Meanwhile, Rommel had realised there were gaps opening on this Australian-held sector and at 11.00 a.m. he directed the 15th Panzer Group (tanks) on to the battlefield. They were to be supported by one regiment of his elite German 164th Light

Division Infantry—foot soldiers delegated to march behind the tanks to assist in both clearing and mopping up.

Herb was watching the tanks approaching D Company when all hell broke loose again as the Allied artillery released a terrific bombardment, aimed at the tanks. The noise was deafening as a deadly duel between the tanks and artillery erupted and was played out less than a few hundred metres from Herb. Eventually, to Herb's relief, the tanks were temporarily forced to withdraw.

By now, the platoon realised they had captured a lot more than soldiers from their earlier action; they had also attained trucks, tanks, weapons and food supplies. The Italians had previously captured some supplies from the retreating British troops and Herb was intrigued to notice some soft drinks which had been manufactured by the Australian firm Cottees on one of the trucks. An extra bonus was that the company cook was able to serve a special appetising lunch created mainly from scrounged Italian rations.

After lunch, at about 2.30, without warning and accompanied by a huge cloud of dust and noise, the Panzer tanks reappeared. Herb noticed them approaching over a small rise, once again moving towards D Company. After a brief skirmish, fighting their way under the Allied artillery fire, the tanks and their supporting infantry had regrouped and were now counter-attacking. This time they were clearly coming Herb's way.

Herb could see they were Rommel's star performers, the 25-ton Panzer IVs, which were readily nicknamed 'Tigers' by the Allies. They were classed as a general-purpose medium tank and were fast and mobile, ideal for desert warfare with its flat, open terrain. They carried a deadly 75-mm turret gun that enabled them to effectively take on machine-gun nests, infantry and anti-tank guns.

Herb hadn't really seen tanks in battle yet. There had

been tank actions at Tobruk, but he had missed them. Now he found them, simply, quite terrifying—and they were charging towards him.

But before the tanks arrived, another threat made life difficult for Herb and D Company. The Stukas reappeared, this time numbering about 60 dive bombers in the formation. The planes peeled off, four at a time. With engines roaring, they would turn on their backs then scream down towards the battlefield, sirens emitting their intimidating wail.

Herb ducked instinctively. The bombs landed all round D Company's positions, some dropping and exploding dangerously close to Herb's piece of ground. Dirt and rock sprayed skyward, but in a miraculous ten minutes of madness not one man was hit. It was about their third attack that day, and Herb knew the Stukas would be back. But right now, he had the advancing tanks to contend with.

Herb's 4 Section, along with another section of 17 Platoon—about 25 men altogether—were in the front line facing the Panzers. It was a chilling sight. Ten massive clanking machines, like so many mythical monsters, were bearing down out of the dust and charging towards them. They were accompanied by infantry soldiers walking behind and to the side of the tanks.

Somebody yelled, 'Better start digging. Here come the Tigers.'

Herb needed no second call. The ground was shaley and hard here, but he dug furiously. It was all he could do to desperately fashion a shallow slit trench for himself—a mere 40 centimetres deep. He jumped in and, lying on his stomach at full length, put his .303 rifle to his shoulder and contemplated the approaching odious shapes.

He could smell the black exhaust flames spewing from the growling diesel engines and could hear the unnerving clanging of the caterpillar treads as they charged relentlessly through the dusty, stark landscape towards him. He began firing, as did every other man in the platoon.

His aim was deadly. He did not want to miss now. The Bren gunner from Herb's section, Bernie Lang, was particularly effective. German soldiers fell between the tanks as Herb's platoon set up a withering wall of fire. Their assault was decisive enough; the German infantry were stopped in their tracks. The soldiers turned and retreated to safer ground, leaving a great number of their compatriots dead and wounded in the field. However, the fire wasn't enough to turn the tanks.

Within minutes the tanks were among the men from the 2/48th. Herb could only stare as the behemoths raced at the front row of slit trenches and attempted to run over and crush the men within them. Herb and his platoon members sprawled as flat as they could, like rats in a hole. Herb watched in horror as the tanks crossed and recrossed the trenches. Ghastly muffled screams from injured and dying men filtered through the sound of the roaring motors. To his horror, Herb noticed several of the tanks were locking one track briefly so the other track would spin and scrape over a trench, pulverising the inhabitants.

Herb watched as one colossus turned and advanced towards him. There was nowhere to go. Terrified, he ducked and flattened himself as much as possible into his trench and braced himself. As the caterpillar track hit his foxhole, he instantly felt the intense pressure bearing down on his spine. It was overwhelming. He could feel the life being crushed out of his ribs and back; hardly breathing, he prayed the walls would hold.

Mercifully, the tank commander didn't spin or grind the tracks, but the sheer weight was sickening. Thankfully also, the tank didn't remain there; it kept moving. Yet to Herb, the few seconds that a section of the track remained stationary above him while its drive wheels turned inside it, seemed like a lifetime.

Eventually, the Panzer rolled away. Herb gasped deeply for breath, sucking in lung fulls of dusty air. He coughed but he forced himself not to panic, slowly dragging the air back into his lungs. Within seconds, the revitalising oxygen entered his brain. He tried desperately to regain his senses; the monster could come back. After a brief assessment, he considered his injuries might only be superficial bruising, although he couldn't easily tell if he had sustained anything more serious. He lifted his head in time to see the tank in the process of running over and crumpling the trench next to him. It was occupied by his mate, Lofty Whaite. Herb could only watch and hope Whaite would survive.

Whaite did survive, suffering the same ignominious fate as Herb. His haversack had been pushed into his back and he was also badly bruised, but otherwise apparently uninjured, his sense of humour certainly still intact. After the tank had rolled away, Whaite shakily stood up, spraying the earth off his back with some pantomime, spluttering and yelling in mock defiance after the beast, 'I don't know why I don't turn that bastard over!'

The ridiculousness of the comment broke the tension; Whaite's sense of timing was perfect. Herb laughed, the action releasing his own anxieties and lifting his spirits. The other men in the platoon also rallied. One man, Sergeant Haynes, another friend of Herb's from Mount Gambier, jumped out of his trench and audaciously raced after the tank. Stalking the machine and cowering low beneath the tank commander's field of vision and its probing machine guns, he slapped a sticky bomb on the side of the tank.

(A 'sticky' bomb—more correctly, the British hand grenade No. 74—consisted of a glass ball on the end of a bakelite handle. Inside was an explosive filling, while the outside consisted of a very sticky adhesive covering, similar to bitumen, which was protected by a metal outer casing. After removing the outer casing, the 1-kilogram bomb is placed or thrown on to the tank, where it was designed to stick in place. After priming the detonator, the soldier has five seconds to get out of harm's way.)

The sergeant dived for cover, but he was too late. Fire from an accompanying tank machine gun ripped through his body, and he fell wounded. Meanwhile, the tank burst into flames. Within seconds, the hatch flew open and some of the crew tried desperately to escape the raging inferno. Such was the anger of the trench inhabitants that no mercy was shown; the Germans were killed instantly in a hail of bullets.

By now, the Allied anti-tank guns and artillery had found the range of the tanks. Intense firepower from these weapons forced the remaining tanks to retreat. However, there wasn't much time for Herb to recover. The tanks had no sooner departed than Rommel's artillery plastered C and D companies' positions again. Herb kept low in his trench as the earth erupted around him once more. The Germans were obviously planning another attack; this was the softening up.

The bombardment kept up for two hours, creating large clouds of dust and smoke. Herb covered his head and ears and curled up in his trench, willing the shells not to land on him. Between bursts, he would shrug the dirt off himself, gasp for air and desperately try to calm himself. This phase of war was as much about acquiring detachment and mental toughness as it was about exhibiting strong physical resolve.

Then the tanks returned. Racing in at about 40 km/h, they encircled C Company first where they met stiff resistance and lost some tanks, then raced back over to Herb's two sections at the front of D Company's positions. Once again, they drove around and over the same slit trenches, but this time the men retaliated with fierce determination. Even though tanks support each other with murderous crossfire from their machine guns, many of the men were prepared to brave this prospect to place sticky bombs on the rampaging machines and destroy them, in the process taking several tank crew members prisoner.

Supporting this assault on the tanks were a troop of anti-tank guns from the 2/3rd Anti-Tank Regiment and a platoon of Vickers machine-gunners from the 2/2nd Machine Gun Battalion. The machine-gunners had dug in slightly to the west of Tel el Eisa Station, about 300 metres south of the railway line. They were just on the left flank of the 2/48th Battalion and from here they poured a lethal fire at the tanks.

The Vickers was known as a medium machine gun and required two men to operate it. It was water-cooled, holding 7 pints of water in the jacket around the barrel, and was heavy, weighing 94 pounds (about 43 kilograms). For action, it was set up on a tripod with one man sitting behind the trigger and the other assisting by feeding the ammunition through the gun. Herb witnessed one encounter which impressed him.

One of the rampaging tanks singled out a Vickers gun position manned by two of the machine-gunners. The tank commander drew up to the trench and demanded that the men surrender, but they resisted and compacted themselves into the bottom of their gun pit. Luckily, they were just out of reach of the tank's machine guns, which could not be depressed enough.

An instant later, the tank itself came under fire from a broadside from the 2/3rd Anti-Tank Regiment. One of the 2-pound shells claimed the tank, knocking it out of action. Another beside it was also destroyed. The roles were now reversed; the German crew jumped out of the tank and attempted to escape to their own lines.

But the sergeant commanding the Vickers team, Gus Longhurst, had other ideas. Their guns were set up behind a slight rise, so Longhurst, a strong rugby forward, jumped to one of the guns, knocked out the pins fixing it to the tripod and lifted it to his waist. He then cradled the weapon to his left hip and fired the thumb-piece trigger with his right hand, a difficult act. With one man feeding the ammunition belt and another soldier helping to steady the recoil, Longhurst fired about 150 rounds at the fleeing tank crew. Two of the Germans fell, seriously wounded; the rest surrendered. Displaying great humanity, Longhurst then tended to the wounds of his fallen enemy, using his own field dressing. The gesture made a strong impression on all who witnessed it, including Herb. It was possible to show compassion to your foe. Herb later heard that Longhurst was awarded an immediate Military Medal for his gallantry.

Now, in the fading evening light, the remaining tanks pulled back, mauled beyond belief by the Australian infantrymen and artillery. But the action wasn't over for the day. The tanks had only retreated just beyond the railway line and, as dusk fell, D Company was aware it was completely covered by the tanks' guns.

Night fell, and soon it became pitch black. The firing quietened and, for some hours, the men nervously listened and peered into the stygian darkness. The silence held for a time, but eventually the distant clanging of hinged metal and diesel throated murmurs heralded the tanks' unwelcome approach. It was terrifying. Herb couldn't see them, but he could hear them squealing and belching, drawing closer. Like phantoms, the tanks crisscrossed over the battlefield again, causing a great deal of noise, fear and confusion.

Lieutenant Smith called Herb to his side, saying, 'It's pretty hopeless here. We're overrun and can't get a fair go at them. They'll eventually wipe us out. I want you to get back to Company Headquarters and find out what we should do: stay here or withdraw.'

Herb assumed an alert crouch posture and half crawled, half crept, keeping low to the ground. In the dark, he was keenly aware it would be difficult to separate friend from foe if he encountered someone. In that instant, he would be allowed only a fleeting second to distinguish the only clearly discernable difference—helmet shape: the Germans wore a basic square shape whereas the Allied helmets were designed more like a saucer.

Luckily, he didn't have to make a decision this time. He found his way to Company Headquarters and relayed the message to the company commander, Captain Williams. The captain's instructions were clear: 'Tell Smithy I want him back from where he is. I'm going to line everybody up behind the railway line; we'll form a new line and attack from there. When he's coming out, tell him not to fire a shot. If he comes across a German, bayonet him. I don't want the Germans to know you're pulling out. Don't pull a trigger—they'll know where we are and send their tanks in. I want to surprise them.'

Herb returned to his platoon and relayed the message to Lieutenant Smith. At about 9.00 p.m., Smith moved quickly and quietly to extricate his men. The retreat was efficient and mercifully uneventful. It was with some relief that, as they moved back, they passed some members of A Company also on their way to the railway line. (A Company was to form a higher line for the impending attack on the tanks.)

A few minutes later, A and D companies were on their start lines, ready to do battle once again. This was fast becoming what Herb thought must be his longest day. (He was wrong; there would be longer ones.) The plan was for A Company to lead, with both companies converging to surround the tanks and all platoons synchronising to simultaneously charge the enemy.

Stealthily, the shadowy forms of the Australian soldiers crept around and closer to the dark shapes of the tanks, silhouetted against the lighter sky. It was the enemy's turn to be nervous. And indeed they were. Suddenly, a startled German released a burst from his Spandau. That was it. The men from the 2/48th stood up and bayonet charged the enemy infantry, running directly at the tanks.

Letting loose with their now well-oiled screaming war cry, the Australians completely intimidated and unnerved the tank crews and infantrymen. Their wild screeches were magnified by the still night air as the sound seemingly emanated from all directions, further unsettling the enemy.

How many Australians were there? The chatter from the Australian Bren guns, Tommy guns, the explosions from grenades and the shrills of the blood-curdling howls resonated right around the enclosure. To the Germans, it seemed like thousands. Panic ensued.

The tank commanders started their tanks, revving their motors and wildly slewing their machines across the desert in an attempt to escape the dangerous threat promised by the hideous cries of these banshees racing among them.

The German infantry attempted to follow, but were met by the determined Australian charge. Enveloped by the dark, the battle was fought at close range. Often too close to shoot, the fight deteriorated into a gritty hand-to-hand contest using bayonets and fists. Men fought desperately like animals, grappling, stabbing, slashing . . . dying.

In the confusion, men from both armies were run over by the retreating tanks or were wounded by the wild firing. Herb saw one man he knew from the battalion killed as he stopped to attend to his jammed Bren gun. However, it was clear even through the dark and the confusion that the Australians had the upper hand. Men such as Sergeant Derrick of 8 Platoon displayed exemplary leadership and courage, Derrick having placed sticky bombs on two tanks, sending gushes of flames spiralling and dancing into the dark night air, and eerily illuminating macabre shadows of men either locked in battle or rolling and fighting to the death in the sand.

But the attack was costly for Herb's 17 Platoon. As he and his friends raced from tank to tank, shooting and screaming as part of the foray, they came into an aggressive firefight with some resistant German infantry. Herb fought fiercely, firing at the silhouettes of square helmets and thrusting at darkened German forms. But during the confusion, the sheer force of German numbers pushed 17 and 18 platoons into a vulnerable situation and, in the blackness, some men became separated. One section of 18 Platoon and another of 17 Platoon were desperately overrun and lost contact. About thirteen men were taken prisoner.

Overall, however, the pressure was telling on the Germans, the audacity and strength of the Australian commitment eventually forcing them into retreat. Herb noticed once again the Germans had an aversion to the prospect of fighting with cold steel. Amid guttural yells from the German commanders, the tanks whirled off the battlefield, grinding away into the darkness, intently followed by their already retreating support troops who dragged their prisoners along with them.

The battle had been short and vicious, but the Australians had regained the Tel el Eisa Railway Station territory. Now they would need to consolidate.

Rommel's nose had well and truly been bloodied by his first stoush with the Australians. During this long and hard day's fighting, the enemy had lost at least eighteen Panzer tanks, 100 German and 850 Italian soldiers imprisoned as well as a large haul of artillery, weapons and equipment. The field was littered with their dead. Against this, the Australians had lost six killed. And they had held onto the Hill of Jesus and the slopes of the Tel el Eisa Railway Station—both critically important strategic positions.

Another boost for the day was achieved by the 2/24th Battalion, when they overran a German position occupied by

Rommel's wireless intercept unit. Most of the German defenders valiantly died protecting the unit's secrets, but the battalion nevertheless captured vital records and code books. Early the next day, Herb noticed several vans being filled with papers, cabinets and files, and was told the information was being sent to London to the code-breakers intelligence unit. Herb eventually found out the code breakers used the files to intercept Hitler's messages to his armies, a fact which authorities credit with shortening the war.

(Of interest to Herb, the captured German colonel in charge of the documents was named Seebohn. Herb wondered whether Seebohn might be a relation since his mother's maiden name was Seebohn. A great number of residents from the Mount Gambier area were of German origin.)

At the end of this day, D Company moved back to the Hill of Jesus where they dug in, while A Company occupied the area around Tel el Eisa Station. In the meantime, the 2/24th Battalion had captured Point 33, and were preparing to attack the slopes of Tel el Eisa itself. Herb considered there might be a chance for a breather. He was absolutely physically and mentally exhausted. But Rommel had other plans. As did Hammer.

SEVEN

Hill of Jesus

In a frantic effort to guard against further disastrous tank attacks, the men of the 2/48th Battalion worked most of the next day and night digging weapon pits and laying mines in front of the battalion's positions. Then, on the morning of 12 July, the battalion endured a terrific shelling. The enemy was going to give them little peace.

Herb was standing next to his trench when he suddenly heard the dreaded *whiisht*. There was nothing he could do. An instant later, the first shells landed. The force knocked him flat to the ground and was accompanied by a deafening explosion which threatened to concuss him. The blast was so violent that the earth trembled and rose on impact. With each strike, men would be lifted clear out of their gun pits and crashed back to earth, left sprawling in the grit. Sand and dust billowed through the air, choking lungs and blinding eyes.

Most of this damage was created by the heavy flak from the 88-mm artillery guns. Originally designed to track fast-moving aircraft, in the desert this weapon's most potent role was in knocking out slow-moving tanks, and it could do so at very long range. With an effective horizontal range of about 10.5 kilometres and perfect optics, it required six crew members to operate it. The crew painted white rings on the barrel, like notches on a gunslinger's six-shooter, to tally the number of tanks the weapon had destroyed. As Herb well knew, infantry were powerless against it.

To add to the torment, many of the shells were airburst, detonating some metres off the ground and spraying lethal shrapnel that would whistle across a wide parameter. The shrapnel inflicted many casualties as the shallow weapon pits did not afford great protection. Men hurriedly acquired sandbags and pieces of old iron for cover, and huddled in their personal 'dungeons'.

This was Rommel's 'softening-up' process. The pounding continued for the next few days with the pattern complemented by Stuka and high-level bomber attacks. The Stuka pilots impressed Herb with their skill as they screeched in low over their targets. From Herb's position, they appeared to be aiming directly at him, but mercifully the bombs actually veered off at an angle before striking the earth. Once again, swirling dust, smoke and fumes filled the air.

Herb was becoming increasingly traumatised by the continual bombardment and general sleep deprivation. In fact, most of the platoon were becoming disorientated and dazed—'bomb happy', as it became known. Some of the men would stagger out of their trenches and wander aimlessly, virtually punch-drunk. They would have to be led back to their trenches.

Herb's friend Lofty Whaite was so badly shocked, he no longer knew where he was. It was disturbing to see this otherwise jovial friend, a blond poet with a sensitive artistic streak, jarred out of his senses, his normal 6-foot frame a crumpled shell. Herb sent him to the battalion doctor, who referred him to the cookhouse for two hours' reprieve. It wasn't anywhere near enough time. Herb noticed he was still stunned, staring vacantly into space on his return.

In fact, there were rumours from other regiments along the line that some men were actually wounding themselves in an effort to be spirited out of this hellhole. Herb empathised; the temptation was there. The bombardments settled a little by 14 July, but during the early hours of that morning 2/48th Battalion was again subjected to a terrific holocaust. Shellfire, followed quickly by a vicious bombing raid which blotted the area with dust and curling smoke, was succeeded by a large force of Panzer III tanks moving to within 100 metres of the battalion. As the tanks advanced, the Australian artillery and anti-tank guns pounded them with intense fire. The AIF's 2/3rd Anti-Tank Regiment's main weapon was the 2-pounder gun. It was not as efficient or as powerful as the Germans' 88 mm but, despite its weakness, at close range it could be every bit as devastating. Three tanks burst into flames, their crews trapped inside. Herb imagined it would be a nasty death, with fear, claustrophobia and panic ruling the men's last seconds on earth.

The remaining tanks rushing at the forward companies of the battalion were greeted by an inferno of sound and fire. The desert erupted as machine guns, anti-tank guns and rifles traded punches with the rampaging machines. One by one, the tanks were cut down. Then, as suddenly as they came, the tanks withdrew, leaving behind ten burnt-out metal hulks, the 2/3rd Anti-Tank Regiment claiming seven of the ten for the loss of one of their guns. Sad ribbons of black smoke spiralled skywards, testament to the Australians' commitment.

The next day, Herb witnessed his first full-on tank battle. In the early morning, the clanking of German tanks was heard behind the cover of pre-dawn darkness and then, as the light intensified, 40 large Panzers were seen advancing towards Point 33. Almost immediately, Herb noticed a squadron of fourteen British Crusader tanks racing to meet them. With a great deal of throttling and roaring from the 54 powerful engines, desperate squealing as their crews violently applied their turning brakes, and intense firing from both groups of tanks and from the Allied artillery (particularly the 2/3rd Anti-Tank Regiment who had joined in), an epic battle was played out in front of Herb's eyes.

The Crusaders, or Cruiser Mark VI tanks, were armed with diminutive 2-pounder guns and were only really effective against the Panzers at close range. So the main tactic for them was to gain as close an access as possible to the enemy while keeping clear of the Panzers' more powerful guns. This required skill, courage and the ability to use the Crusader tank's greater mobility to advantage.

Dust and smoke once again filled the air and the smell of cordite and diesel fumes fell heavily over the desert sands. The roaring of the clash of titans was compelling. Herb looked on, mesmerised. The battle raged for some hours, with the occasional sound of an exploding tank punctuating the general background cacophony. Eventually, the Panzers were forced to withdraw under the onslaught of the combined forces. More derelict and burnt-out tanks were left fuming on the landscape as the remaining tanks were driven off.

But they returned again that evening, along with motor transports and troops. The mines in front of the battalion's positions accounted for several tanks and vehicles, but the rest met a deadly hail of fire and grenades. Enemy infantry charged in the dark, but they were clearly silhouetted against their burning tanks and vehicles. Not one soldier made the nearest 2/48th post; they were all stopped, slaughtered by deadly fire from machine guns and rifles. Once again, the tanks and remaining infantry retreated, leaving the field scattered with their dead.

For the men of 2/48th Battalion, there was no real respite from the continued attrition, although on 16 July, Rommel was forced to turn his attention to the Tel el Eisa feature itself. In the early morning, two companies of the 2/23rd Battalion and five tanks brilliantly took both East Point 24 and West Point 24 of the *tel*. However, Rommel brought up large columns of reinforcements and concentrated intense and accurate artillery mortar and machine-gun fire against the position. By 11.30 a.m. the aggressive assault decimated the Australians, killing and wounding 90 of the 200 soldiers.

Realising the situation was untenable, the survivors of the 2/23rd Battalion withdrew, leaving Tel el Eisa once again in German hands. The Eighth Army needed the height of Tel el Eisa. From here, Point 24 (at 24 feet) had commanding views of the battlefield and the Mediterranean Sea. This would set the scene for the 2/48th challenge to follow.

The large numbers of dead—predominantly Germans—left lying to rot in no-man's-land was presenting a potential health problem. After a few days of lying under the 40°-plus sun, the bodies would swell, the result of bacteria invading the tissues and accelerating decomposition and putrefactive changes. The stench of death was beginning to waft and penetrate among the living, suffocating soldiers in their trenches.

Flies made no distinction between dead bodies and food utensils, precipitating concern about the spread of disease. Herb was selected to be part of a burial party to venture into no-man's-land under the cover of darkness. The men were issued with gas masks as the odour was so offensive. The task was gruesome. One man was elected to stand guard while the others moved among the bodies.

Herb noticed most bodies were bloated and their features grossly distorted, the abdomen assuming a marbled green colour. Dark red and green putrid bubbling fluid oozed from the mouth and nostrils. Some abdomens were distended and swollen to about 70 centimetres in height, and were festering with maggots. They would have to be let down. A sharp bayonet thrust emitted a foul smelling gas, deflating the corpse.

The aim of the burial was to simply consign the bodies to a

shallow grave and cover them; there would be no headstone, or cross. To Herb's horror, occasionally a cadaver would be so decomposed that a limb would pull off in his hand. It was a grotesque mission, made even more macabre in the dark. Some of the squad were so repulsed by the grisly undertaking they vomited. Herb undertook several of these excursions over the next week or so as the battalion remained entrenched on the Hill of Jesus. The cruel irony that such atrocious events should occur at a site associated with a prophet who preached peace and love was not lost on some of the men.

Another night mission Herb took part in during this period was patrolling to capture an enemy for interrogation purposes. The ongoing military situation was so knife-edged that head-quarters needed constant information in order to keep the enemy at bay. The simplest technique was the opportunist method he employed so many times at Tobruk. That is, a squad of two would lie in wait in no-man's-land and intercept a German patrol.

When the patrol had gone past, the two men would move up, one each side of the 'tail-end Charlie'—the last man of the patrol—and aim their rifles at him. They would quietly indicate he was to come back, quickly. Generally, there was no place for heroics for the German; it would be obvious he and his colleagues would be quickly killed if he did not comply.

The other method was for a squad of about six men to hide either side of a path that a German patrol was known to take. Two soldiers would be delegated to pinpoint an intended prisoner and hide in wait. The German patrol would then be ambushed and, while the main troop would be involved in a fire fight, the two soldiers would race in and secure their prisoner.

One night shortly after the tank battle, Herb was intrigued to hear engines out in front of the 2/48th Battalion's position. He was sure they weren't tanks and they didn't sound like trucks. A Verey flare went up and revealed a heavy tractor towing a large platform around the battlefield. It pulled up beside a damaged tank and mechanics hopped off and raced around the vehicle, attaching it to a powerful winch. Incredibly, the tank was lifted onto the platform and quickly moved away into the darkness.

Herb wondered why no one fired at the tractor, but he imagined the artillery was loath to give away their positions for this event. The point is that Rommel had lost a large number of tanks in this troublesome northern sector and needed to resurrect every available machine.

During these two weeks while the 2/48th were at the Hill of Jesus, other brigades and divisions countered Rommel right along the El Alamein Line. On 15 July, the New Zealand Division and the 5th Indian Regiment carried out strikes at Ruweisat Ridge, 10 kilometres south of El Alamein Station.

The battle resulted in one New Zealand brigade being completely overrun with the shocking loss of 1405 men killed, wounded or captured.

On 17 July, the Australian 9th Division sent the 24th Brigade to strike at Makh Khad Ridge. Over two days they captured and held the ridge. Other engagements by other divisions kept the front alive and seething with action and noise.

Basically, during this period, both sides sparred and hunted for an opening, each commander looking for a knock-out blow. With each punch thrown, a strong counter-punch was always the answer. While both generals searched for a breakthrough, Hitler and Churchill pressed for a victory. However, the overall position remained static.

What was important, however, was that the Australian tenacity in the north prevented Rommel from creating a chance to outflank the British in the south. Once again, the Australians proved themselves a thorn in Rommel's side.

This was the situation as 22 July dawned. This was to be Herb's longest day.

EIGHT
Tel el Eisa

On this day, 22 July, the soldiers of the Desert Eighth Army had been briefed to prepare for a general attack.

Auchinleck was mindful that Churchill was under political pressure at home and that the Allies still desperately needed a significant victory. He planned for a major offensive to commence in the early hours of that day. The 2nd New Zealand Division, two brigades strong, was to attack El Mreir, south of Ruweisat Ridge, the 161st Indian Brigade was to fight along Ruweisat Ridge itself and the 1st South African Division was to move on the Indian brigade's right flank.

The Australian 9th Division was to take Tel el Eisa Ridge and the dominating ridge behind that feature. For the 26th Brigade, the 2/48th Battalion was to seize West Point 24 of the *tel*, while its sister battalion, the 2/23rd, was to capture East Point 24. The third battalion of the brigade, the 2/24th, was to capture an objective on Ring Contour 25. In the meantime, the 24th Brigade was to take the feature behind Tel el Eisa.

The detailed plan was complicated and Lieutenant-General Morshead, the General Officer Commanding AIF, objected to the scope of the Australians' responsibilities. He was concerned about the risk of casualties and the uncertainty of success. This sentiment was echoed down the line. By the time it had reached Herb and the men in 17 Platoon, there was great disquiet.

Herb found out on the evening of 21st July. Lieutenant Smith approached him and said, 'Herb, come over to Company Headquarters with me.'

'What for?' Privates don't usually go to Company Headquarters with brass.

'You'll find out when we get there.'

Along with all the officers and the NCOs (non-commissioned officers) of D Company, Herb realised he was going to be privy to a briefing. The company commander, Captain Colin Williams, informed them in some detail of D Company's role in the action for the next day.

'Tomorrow, first thing, we are to take Tel el Eisa. First though, two companies from one of our sister battalions, the 2/24th, are to attack Ring Contour 25, about a thousand yards northwest of the Hill of Jesus, and one company from our other sister battalion, the 2/23rd, is to take East Point 24 of Tel el Eisa. When they have secured this, our D Company and B Company will pass through the 2/23rd and we will take West Point 24. Our main task, in effect, is to block the enemy's supply line to their main headquarters area as well as to Mersa Matruh, Tobruk and Tripoli.'

After delivering a number of directions, he said to Herb, 'There's not time to make you a corporal. As of now, you're an acting corporal, and you're going to lead a section tomorrow. I know you're in 4 Section, but I'm making you leader of 5 Section. Their corporal was taken prisoner yesterday.'

'Am I?' Herb asked, surprised.

'Yes.' Case closed.

Williams continued. 'One of the problems with the attack is that it will be in daylight. It could be a problem. We know that opposite us is the German 90th Light Division [90 Leichte Afrika Division]. It's one of Rommel's crack units and we'll be in for a tough fight whatever happens. Tack has complained to the top brass and it's gone higher, but I don't think it'll do much good. So I'll see you all tomorrow morning—early!'

Herb realised there was no point arguing with the captain. He now had rank and his stomach twisted into a nice tight knot. About 10 p.m. he returned to 17 Platoon and rounded up the ten men of 5 Section. Controlling his own innate fears and addressing them in a confident voice, he said, 'Right, you fellows, I've just been made an acting corporal—in charge of this section. Know something?'

There were general congratulations all round. In answer to his question, the response was a collective 'No.'

'We're to go in tomorrow morning and take this position.' Herb pointed to the map, West Point 24 on Tel el Eisa. 'I'm leading you buggers in.'

'No. That's bloody terrible.' Several men echoed the thoughts of the section. 'That'll be suicide, in daylight. We'd be mad to do that.'

'Well, Tack tried to talk sense into the top command, but we still have to go.'

There was much argumentative discussion concerning the mission and the possible outcomes. Herb realised nobody would sleep, including himself, so he decided he should keep them occupied by talking about it.

'You'd better all wear your helmets. It may save your life; a bullet won't go through a tin hat,' he said.

The men started arguing about that possibility; Herb knew they would debate over anything. 'Yes, it will go through,' some said.

'No, it won't,' others disagreed.

He kept them distracted in this manner for many hours. Eventually, before dawn, they were snapped into reality by the thunder of the Allied 25-pounders artillery breaking the silence of the night.

'It's started,' Herb said, looking at the flashes of flame as they danced across the darkened desert horizon.

'All hell should break loose soon. The 2/23rd and 2/24th will be going in now. Grab a stockpile of ammo and then let's move.' As B and D companies made their way down off the coastal ridge slopes of the Hill of Jesus to the starting point at Tel el Eisa Station, the wicked whisper of German shells countering the attack whined overhead. The men waited beside the railway line as the sound of vicious battle echoed all around them.

Just as the sun was throwing its first streak of light over the troubled landscape, a few minutes before 6.00 a.m., the men from B and D companies received word that the other battalions, the 2/23rd and 2/24th, had achieved their objectives. In fact, as the intensity of the sound and flashes had reflected, both battalions had been involved in a tremendous fight. Both battlefields had resulted in a great number of casualties, to the extent that the 2/23rd's hold on West Point 24 of Tel el Eisa was extremely tenuous. However, the signal had been sent; B and D companies moved off their start line.

The timing of the advance was staggered so that individual platoons could proceed in turn. By the time 5 Section had moved off, the rising sun had gained considerable intensity. To the men's frustration, it framed them like a beacon.

'Blast,' thought Herb. 'This is madness. We should have gone at night.' Herb felt distinctly uneasy. He was now placed in a leadership role with responsibility for ten men in his section as well as two engineers who were to assist with dismantling any mines they might encounter.

D Company was programmed to head direct to West Point 24 while B Company swung away to approach from the left flank. By the time the forward platoons of D Company had gone about a kilometre and Herb's section had moved about a half a kilometre from the railway line, they all came under sudden intense and accurate fire.

'It's on,' Herb called to his men. 'Keep your formation.' Machine-gun fire cut a deadly swathe across the forward platoons. In the stillness of the morning air, the rattling of Spandaus echoed like cannon. The assault was followed instantly by an 88-mm gun firing airburst shells at them. The shells exploded at about a metre above the ground, spraying vicious shrapnel over the battlefield. More men dropped and rolled among the camel thorn and sand; for some, their final resting place.

A direct hit destroyed D Company's radio. Communication was going to be difficult. Already, some key officers had been killed. Herb's section didn't falter. Methodically, as well-trained and disciplined soldiers, they steadily moved through the hail of bullets, smoke, dust and explosions, rifles at the ready.

To add to the confusion, Herb noticed men streaming back from the Tel el Eisa area, moving through D Company. Many of them were wounded, all exhausted. They were soldiers of the 2/23rd Battalion and had been subjected to an intense and cruel enemy fire. Gradually they were being pushed off West Point 24; their tennous hold was cracking. Over to the right, the 2/24th at Ring Contour 25 were also beginning to feel Rommel's pressure; they too were withdrawing.

Suddenly, in the midst of the tumult, Lieutenant Jim Smith appeared, racing between sections.

'Herb,' he said, 'the whole company is going to go in—up the middle. We're copping plenty of casualties. We've lost almost all our officers, including Captain Williams. He was killed a while ago. I think I'm the last one. I want you to take your section around to the ridge over to the left side and give covering fire.' Smith pointed to a rise to the side of the main action, about a metre high, overlooking the battle site. It would protect

the main company thrust moving up towards the slopes of Tel
el Eisa.

Those were Smith's last words. He had no sooner moved
back towards the other sections of his platoon when he dropped
to the ground, riddled with machine-gun bullets. He was seriously wounded, the murderous spray ripping holes across his
chest and penetrating his lungs. Blood gurgled from his mouth
and his chest; he was out of the quest, the last officer. The six
officers from D Company were all gone.

Herb noticed other men race to the scene, supporting Smith
and making him comfortable. Herb was shocked at Smith's
sudden fall, a man he liked and had great respect for. It was
never easy losing friends. It's the suddenness and the degree of
violence that is difficult to comprehend. Herb had to force the
image out of his mind.

He had been given an order and he realised Smith was in the
best possible hands. He called to his men, 'At the double. We're
going around behind that rise. We're to give support to the main
company who are going up the middle.' Herb, running now,
briskly led his men forward and around to the left-hand side of
the main action. In a few minutes, they approached the small
rise from behind.

'Hang on,' he signalled quietly. 'Look, there's about a half-
dozen Germans lying doggo on the rise we're after, in
trenches—firing at our men. We'll have to get rid of them. Pick
a man and shoot on my command.'

Herb aimed at the closest German. 'Now, fire,' he called. A
fusillade of flame and smoke poured from thirteen weapons.
The Germans had been caught and surprised. Herb watched as
his target instantly fell forward, dropping his weapon, a circular
stain of blood appearing over his shoulder blade. Several others
collapsed and crumpled where they were shot. A couple twisted
and began recklessly firing back at Herb's men, who by now

were sprinting towards the entrenchments. Bayonets glinted in the early morning sun. With deadly skill and lightning speed, the crunch and thrust of steel slicing against bone emitted a sickening sound. A few seconds later, the German soldiers were all dead.

Briskly, the bodies were unceremoniously lifted out of their trenches and laid to the side. Six of Herb's men jumped in and replaced the Germans' positions while the remaining seven lay on the ground and set up a killing field.

Over the brim of the rise, he could clearly see the enemy were set up opposite them in strong positions, most dug into trenches and behind sandbags. He considered there were at least two full companies there, probably up to 300 men. They were at the base of Tel el Eisa and were directly in the path of the advancing 2/48th D Company.

Herb had an advantage: the Germans didn't know he and his section were there. They were remarkably close but well concealed. Some of the nearest German trenches were only about 20 metres' distance and were at an angle facing away from Herb. The Germans were also intensely involved and distracted in directing as much damage as possible to the main body of D Company, raining down a sheet of machine-gun and rifle fire.

Herb could see Australians falling in the front platoons. They were clearly highlighted by the glare of the morning sun, setting themselves up as perfect targets.

'My God,' Herb thought, 'they're going to be slaughtered.' Over the clangour of battle, he yelled, 'Let's give them some protection.'

Each man raised his weapon, took deliberate aim at an enemy soldier, released the safety catch, felt for the first pressure on the trigger and then fired at will. Every weapon loosed its payload as machine-gun and rifle fire filled the air with screaming bullets. The Germans had not seen Herb and his men and had no idea where this extra deluge of metal was coming from.

The hail of lead thumped into the enemy, dropping several close by and eliciting screams from others. The attack generated great confusion as the perplexed and panicked soldiers searched for the perpetrators.

The section's Bren gunner, Ray Bloffwitch, had a field day. Gripping the handle of the Bren and steadying the barrel with the tripod, he fired incessantly in a wicked arc, blasting every living being in its path. Men fell, writhing in agony, cursing the unseen assassin.

Herb, lying a few metres from Bloffwitch, fired and reloaded his .303 as fast as he could. He wasn't shooting rabbits now and he didn't waste any bullets. The expended shells clinked and ripped out from the ejection chamber as he dropped one after another of the enemy. The smell of burnt cordite quickly filled his nostrils, fuelling a now trained murderous response.

Right along the line, the unrelenting and deathly fire from the thirteen men saturated the closest German trenches. Men cursed, shouted, screamed or fell silent as the spinning lead found its mark. Within minutes, about 100 Germans lay dead or wounded.

It was soon obvious the onslaught had created a serious distraction. Several of the Germans stopped firing at the advancing Australian platoons and moved back to safer ground. A few more followed and Herb could see they were in a general state of confusion. He could imagine them thinking, surely this amount of damage could not be attributed to the Australians they could see firing in front of them. Five Section's seclusion could not, of course, last. Eventually, the enemy deduced their general direction, the extreme concentration of firepower and smoke helping to give them away.

The pendulum swung. A number of the entrenched enemy now turned their full attention to Herb and his men. Machine-gun and rifle fire opened up and saturated the small rise. Bullets screamed overhead; some thumped into the front of their trenches; others ricocheted off rocks, emitting a terrible whining sound as they spun and funnelled dangerously out of control, adding to the terror. One of Herb's men slumped forward and grabbed his shoulder, screaming.

Five Section fired back, increasing the pounding crescendo of the thunderous gunfire; the noise was tremendous, even stupefying. An acrid adrenalin-fuelling smell of gunpowder penetrated the air, and smoke and dust made breathing difficult.

Herb kept firing. He would tentatively raise his head through the inferno and shoot above the crest of the rise. Suddenly, his head was jerked backwards. The movement was accompanied by a terrifying clanking sound, ringing through his head and in his ears. He knew instantly a bullet had hit his helmet.

'My God. I've been hit,' he screamed.

At the same instant, his rifle went spinning from his hands, knocked by the same burst of machine-gun fire. Splinters shattered and sprayed from the woodwork, effectively buckling the barrel. The shock momentarily dazed him and he involuntarily stood up, then just as quickly fell to earth again. Concussed and confused, a few seconds passed as he stared vacantly into space. Then, steadily, he began to recover, trying desperately to focus and drag himself back into reality. Before long he grasped his situation and the fact that he was still alive. He quickly carried out a personal assessment. Nothing serious, he thought; everything seems okay. Just a whack in the head.

He took off his helmet and noticed there was a neat small hole where the bullet had hit the rim in front and then entered the helmet. It had spun around inside, the force raising the helmet off his head, then parted his hair without touching his skull. The bullet then emerged from a large 5-centimetre hole where it had smashed its way through the back of the helmet.

Sticking his finger through the hole and laughing, he held the helmet up to show his mates. 'Have a look at this, you bastards.'

He realised how lucky he was that he could still laugh at all.

So much for the discussion the previous evening concerning the value of wearing a helmet.

Herb then examined his rifle and realised it was unserviceable. A few metres away was the body of a dead Australian, one of his mates from the company who had been killed earlier. Herb scrambled over to the man and appropriated his rifle. He then moved back to his position and fired a test shot. It was firing a little to the left, so he rearranged the sights. Now it was accurate. Back to the job.

Unfortunately, during the earlier firefight one of his men was injured—one of the two engineers who were assigned to his section had caught a bullet in his shoulder. Herb was now able to give some attention to the man. He found that he had lost a fair degree of blood, but the bleeding was soon stemmed by a pressure bandage. The man insisted he was alright and continued to hold his position.

In the meantime, B Company, approaching Tel el Eisa from the left flank, weren't faring any better. Within a few moments of leaving the starting point, they also came under heavy fire. The enemy, who had displaced the 2/23rd Battalion from East Point 24, was now adding to the bombardment and firepower, forcing B Company to go to ground within 200 metres of the enemy posts. Very quickly, the withering fire accounted for many men, including all the officers except one. The remaining officer was isolated out on the extreme flank, so the acting sergeant-major, Sergeant Wally Prior, took charge.

By 6.30 a.m., both B and D companies were now forced to ground. There was no safe place in the desert arena. Every square metre was covered and raked by intense machine-gun and shell fire. Any movement was perilous.

Then, about 35 metres across to his right, Herb noticed action from the men from the other two sections of his 17 Platoon. They were on their feet, marching headlong into the maelstrom, virtually leading the company towards Tel el Eisa, all the while being steadily whittled away by the deadly broadside. Herb saw a couple of his friends fall and then, to his disgust, he saw two medical corps men fall also. These men fight and march with the company, wearing only the internationally protected Red Cross symbol and carrying no weapons.

Then one man suddenly decided to change things.

Something snapped in Private Stan Gurney's mind. With his face set like flint, he spontaneously jumped from his walking position and sprinted towards the enemy's lines, bullets whistling all around him. His initiative inspired other men to follow. Bernie Lang, Ivan Hanel, Wally Shane and others sprang to their feet and raced through the inferno, determined to dislodge the entrenched Germans.

Their audacity completely surprised the enemy. Miraculously, none of the charging warriors were hit as they travelled the first 40 metres.

As Gurney approached within metres of the closest machine-gun nest, he slowed his stride for a few seconds, raised his rifle to his shoulder and fired at one of the shocked soldiers. The blast at close range slammed into the man's chest and rotated him like a corkscrew, killing him instantly. Gurney swung his attention to the man beside him, aimed and fired again. The soldier's head was violently jerked forward as the bullet smashed into his throat. The man grabbed for his neck as his precious life-blood seeped over his fingers. It was his last movement before he sank to the ground.

By now, a third German in the nest had sprung to his feet. He was raging with anger and coloured the air with a string of German invectives. He lunged at Gurney. Herb knew Gurney to be very fit—before the war he was a skilled professional cyclist and worked outdoors as an electrician with the Perth Electricity and Gas Depot. He was older than the average enlisted man and, at 33 years, was tagged as 'independent', often showing a spirited disrespect for bureaucratic authority. Herb got on well with him.

His fitness and irrepressible nature showed now. Moving his elbows like pistons, he swung his rifle around to meet his irate aggressor. With a lightning-swift thrust, he plunged the bayonet deep into the German's side. The metal found its mark and the soldier dropped to the ground, paralysed, life ebbing from him.

In the meantime, Bernie Lang, who was only a few steps behind Gurney, was clearing a path with his Bren gun. Herb knew how effective Bernie could be; he was beside him on 10 July when they were being overrun by 'Tiger' tanks and infantry.

Then, to Herb's horror, he saw Lang stumble and fall. As he rolled, it was obvious from the damage and blood that he had been ripped apart by machine-gun bullets.

At the same time, Herb's friend Ivan Hanel, who had arrived with him as a reinforcement at Tobruk, was matching Gurney in his speed and tenacity. He followed Gurney into the machine-gunners' nest and confronted one of the two remaining Germans. The gunner had grabbed his Luger pistol and was about to fire it when Hanel lunged at him with all his strength, plunging his bayonet deep into his chest.

In the meantime, Gurney had withdrawn his bayonet, now red to the hilt, from the crumpled, formerly noisy soldier and turned to attack the final gunner. Standing shoulder to shoulder beside Hanel, he jumped at the man and buried his bayonet deep in the pit of the soldier's stomach. Instantly, he withdrew it, leaving the soldier doubled in agony and clutching at his mid-section, his eyes wide with surprise, fear and pain, then steadily losing focus as they finally stared into infinity.

Gurney jumped out of the nest, then started running towards the next one. But there was a price for this fearless charge. Hanel was about to straighten and follow Gurney when, like Lang, he was cut down by a stream of bullets. He collapsed across the German he had just killed.

Wally Shane, Herb's friend from Spalding who joined up with him, was racing a few metres behind Hanel and was about to follow Gurney. Herb watched helplessly as Shane too was riddled by vicious crossfire. He collapsed and rolled, sprawling in the dust, then lay perfectly still, his eyes closed in death.

Still more men were following. Further across the field and a little forward, Herb noticed 17 Platoon's Sergeant Lin Evans rallying his men and setting a resolute example. Racing towards the enemy position, he was caught in a machine gun's arc of fire. He was hit twice, but kept running. Finally, he also paid the ultimate price as another concerted machine-gun volley knocked him off his feet.

By now, Gurney was almost at the next machine-gunners' nest. Herb noted that Gurney's courageous assault was not only prompting his own men to follow, and indeed the company as a whole was now moving forward with the impetus, but it was also triggering a wave of uncertainty and terror among some of the enemy. In fact, about 30 Germans in the direct path of the rampaging Australians left their trenches and began to move back.

'Let's keep them going,' Herb yelled. The distraction caused by Gurney had also decreased the enemy fire on Herb's section, of which they took full advantage. Herb and his section proceeded to pour intense amounts of lead into the retreating men, cutting down one after another. Herb watched at least a dozen men fall, most of them killed.

Herb then watched as a brave German commander, a captain, stood and roared after his fleeing troops. His threatening words stopped them and the men slowly started to return. The commander presented a perfect target. Herb took careful aim, fired and saw the effect of the bullet as it slammed into his chest. The man dropped to the ground. Herb could see he was severely wounded and it was evident that he would no longer be able to influence the battle.

There was an opportunity for gallantry in this vehement environment; Herb did not finish him off. In fact, he had discussed with his men already, that if they wounded a man seriously enough so that he was out of the action, they were to let him alone.

By now, Gurney had sprinted a further 25 metres and reached a second post. Without slowing, he jumped into it. Frenziedly brandishing his rifle and bayonet as if it was an extension of himself, he created as much havoc in here as he had in the first one. With lightning speed, he garrotted one soldier and then confronted a second who was stunned into inaction by Gurney's audacity. An instant later, he was dead, a victim of the Australian's cut and thrust. A third, sensing the inevitable, threw up his hands in defeat, an act that saved his life. Gurney signalled for him to get out of the trench and pointed to the advancing 2/48th men. In an instant, the German bolted out of the post and, thrusting his hands high in the air, moved back towards the Australian line; anything to be away from this rampaging bull.

But Gurney had not finished. With a leap, he vaulted out of the pit and raced towards a third nest. Drenched in sweat now, his face determined and glistening, his fitness was obvious as his strong thighs slammed his feet into the sandy desert soil, propelling him forward.

By now, the Germans in the third post were well aware of his intentions. They opened up with a Spandau but Gurney's speed and dash interrupted their aim, causing the bullets to whiz harmlessly away from him. Then one soldier threw a stick grenade at him. (This is a grenade which is attached to a handle, or stick, and the fuse ignites only after it is flung from the hands.) It landed directly at Gurney's feet and exploded, raising a cloud of dust and showering the immediate area with rocks and shrapnel.

Herb watched transfixed as the force pulled Gurney up sharp and lifted him completely off his feet. It then somersaulted him onto his backside.

'My God,' Herb yelled. 'He's gone arse-over. Oh no—he's bought it.'

But to Herb's amazement, Gurney sat up, searched for his rifle, picked it up and shakily got to his feet again. Herb had seen stick grenades before. He'd noticed that they don't always kill, but they have the power to knock a person over.

Adrenalin still high and pumping, Gurney moved his legs again and quickly recovered his stride. He had regained control now and within another twenty steps he was at the third machine-gun nest.

He didn't hesitate. With his eyes narrowed and teeth clenched with blind hatred, he jumped into the post and continued his killing spree. Herb could see his trained powerful shoulders pumping like a machine. He was swinging his rifle as if it was a toy. Then, with deliberate intent, he thrust, slashed, drove and weaved with the wicked bayonet. Bright red blood spurted and drenched Gurney and the inhabitants of the nest.

There were at least five soldiers in the pit and Herb could see Gurney vigorously account for several more of the enemy during that ghastly onslaught. Then a single shot rang out. The weight of numbers was eventually too much. The odds gave out. The wild movement stopped. Gurney was finally killed, his courageous attack finished by a single bullet.

Herb wondered at the devastation Gurney had caused. Bodies lay randomly sprawled over a 100-metre pathway. Gurney had probably killed ten men himself but, more importantly, the break-out allowed D Company to continue the advance. By the time the Germans had regrouped, the company had gained valuable ground, being forced to dig in only 150 metres from their objective.

Just as interesting, Herb thought, is the positive change in morale when men witness courageous deeds. Who can say what motivates an individual to risk all for a cause? Whether Gurney charged cloaked in a mantle of his own invincibility or out of desperation for what may have appeared to him to be a last-stand situation, or even whether he simply felt indignant at being pushed too far or repugnant at the enemy killing defenceless medical men; regardless, no one could question his fearlessness.

Some may say men without fear often display a reduced sensitivity and appreciation of life and should be followed with caution. However, there is no denying the difference this type of selfless heroism can make in a battle.

In the meantime, the remnants of the 2/23rd Battalion were still holding on at West Point 24. At about 8.00 a.m. the Germans opened a fierce counterattack and, in the process, pinned down the 2/23rd as well as B and D companies of the 2/48th. Nobody could move.

Lieutenant-Colonel Hammer had by now received reports that his men were being cut to pieces. He ordered Bren carriers forward to relieve his companies, some carrying support weapons, others to carry out the wounded. However, such was the rate of enemy artillery and anti-tank fire that the carriers were quickly turned back. The companies could not be reached this way.

In the meantime, Herb and his section prepared to settle in for the day. By 9.00 a.m. they realised they were virtually surrounded and were not going to be extricated easily. In their favour, however, the Germans still didn't really know how many men Herb had under his command, or even exactly where they were. His troops would fire intermittently, yet sparingly, always inflicting damage. They began to be careful with their ammunition, making sure every shot counted, not knowing how long they would need to hold out.

In fact, Herb was aware that if they tried to crawl out now, they would quickly be shot. This thought also weighed heavily on some of his section. As the sun started to really burn down, a couple of the men said to Herb, 'Maybe we should become prisoners. We're all going to be killed if we stay here, or we'll die of thirst.' Each man only had one water bottle for the mission.

'No way,' Herb replied firmly, incredulous at the suggestion. 'We're here. We're not giving up. Ration your water. We'll stay here all day if we have to.'

In the meantime, many wounded men from the forward companies were still trying to retreat through the following columns. One stumbled onto Herb's section and Herb recognised him as a friend from school days, Bob King. King was in B Company and was carrying a shoulder wound. He was exhausted, thirsty and not in a good way. Herb welcomed him and set him up, passing his own water bottle to him.

At this stage, Hammer had asked for tank support and at 11.00 a.m. nine British Valentine tanks arrived at the railway line.

'We might be okay,' Herb said. 'I can hear our tanks coming for us.'

But there was a delay—a long delay. There was no more immediate movement from the tanks.

The temperature was now building to its normal midday 40°C-plus, and conditions were becoming uncomfortable for both sides. The Germans desperately needed information on Herb's contingent as Herb and his men continued to pour sporadic fire on them, adding to the Germans' misery.

Even though Herb's troops were vigilant, they were forced to keep their heads down most of the time; the tension was exhausting and often invoked somnolence. In one of these periods, two Germans crawled up to the extreme flank of the section and quietly took one of the men prisoner. He was the second of the two engineers assigned to the group.

The first inkling Herb had of the transgression was when he suddenly saw the two Germans marching behind the prisoner. The man had his hands high in the air. To Herb's amazement, they were moving across the front of his protective rise, the Germans obviously not aware of the rest of the hidden section. The engineer was keeping a considerable distance in front of his captors and was leading them towards Herb's quarter, less than 30 metres away. Herb read the message.

In an instant, he signalled to the soldier lying next to him. They would take a German each. On Herb's command, they both took deliberate aim and fired. They could not miss at that range. The Germans fell to the ground, dead. The engineer raced back to the rise, relieved to have regained his freedom and gasping for breath.

Herb passed word along that every man needed to be more alert; to try to stay awake. But the warning was not enough. Not long after, the Germans repeated the same procedure, this time capturing Bob King. Once again, Herb watched in disbelief as King suddenly appeared, leading the Germans along the same route as the engineer had done earlier. Herb nudged the soldier next to him and a few seconds later the two Germans lay dead, sprawled alongside their two compatriots killed earlier. King raced back to Herb and the safety of the ridge. He was quite shaken and visibly disturbed by his close call, particularly as he was already carrying a wound.

'Hell Herb, it's a wonder we're not all being taken prisoner. How are we ever going to get out? I think we're all going to get killed. Maybe we should give up.'

Herb replied, 'No bloody way.' He raised his voice. 'We could get killed either way. We'll stay here and try and get out at night. Just shut up and fight back when you can.' King calmed down, then went back to his spot, determined to hold his position.

A little later, at about 3.00 p.m., the nine Valentine tanks which Herb had heard earlier finally began their move. They had only gone several metres past the railway line when they encountered a small enemy minefield. They withdrew and the commanders had a conference, deciding to resume the attack, but this time skirting the minefield and careering towards Tel el Eisa.

As the three leading tanks approached, it looked to Herb's section as though they might be saved. 'Bewdy!' Up went the cry, 'Here comes the cavalry.' However, the virulent German 88-mm anti-tank gun, the same one that had been firing all day, doing a great deal of damage, changed its aim and commenced an accurate rapid-fire attack on the tanks. It was a formidable weapon capable of firing 20-pound shells at the rate of twenty per minute over some 10 kilometres.

Herb and his men looked on dejectedly as the deadly 88-mm shells claimed three tanks in quick succession. One Valentine exploded in flames, instantly killing the crew. The precise firing knocked the tracks off the other two, effectively immobilising them. The crew members didn't attempt to leave the protection of their tanks as it was obvious they were stranded in the middle of a hotbed of enemy activity. They would sit it out. Meanwhile, three more circles were added to the 88's barrel.

The other six tank commanders quickly sensed the futility of the situation. Eighty-eights can shoot further than tanks and this gun was unerring. The tanks swivelled on their tracks and withdrew from the battlefield.

Almost immediately, the Germans sent out a party of three soldiers to collect the British crewmen from the two crippled tanks.

'Those tanks were our way out of here,' Herb said. 'Let's give it to the bastards.' Herb and his section delivered a tirade of bullets at the soldiers. There was no escape; they all died instantly.

A few minutes later, a second party of Germans was dispatched. Herb waited till they got close to the tanks. 'Again!' Herb yelled. Another round of deadly fire repeated the earlier result, and three more Germans lay dead.

About half an hour later, the enemy tried again. This group was very alert but Herb played his advantage. With all the background gunfire reverberating around the battlefield from the larger conflict, the reports from Herb's rifles were somewhat masked; the Germans were still not completely aware of where this dangerous local fire was coming from. However, the effect was the same: three more Germans lay dead.

However, after this last sortie, the Germans were gaining more knowledge of the direction of Herb's men. They were doing too much damage; they had to go. Some time later, a squad of four Germans crawled towards 5 Section. Herb saw them coming, but waited till they got quite close.

One of the Germans yelled something in broken English. The soldier next to Herb commented, 'Maybe they want us to give up.' Herb knew he still had the upper hand and was determined not to give anything away. He could do a lot more damage yet.

'No bloody way. Let's give it to them,' Herb commanded.

Led by Ray Bloffwitch on the Bren gun, the whole section opened up on the hapless soldiers. Within seconds, the four of them were shredded as bullets ripped their bodies and clothing apart. They joined the growing number of lifeless enemy littered around Herb's immediate combat area.

The day was becoming a test of endurance. The section had brought no food and water was scarce. Herb had given his water bottle away and was starting to feel the effects of dehydration and the stress of the battle. The molten sun gloated. The desert wore the blank look of death.

His concentration lapsed for a few minutes while he put his rifle down and contemplated their position. He was unaware that another group of four Germans was approaching his rise and when he finally looked up he was confronted by a strong-jawed Aryan soldier posturing less than a metre away, pointing a submachine gun directly at his head.

However, the German had been entirely focused on approaching stealthily and was obviously as shocked to suddenly see Herb as Herb was to see him. Both men froze, their eyes riveted. Each man weighed the odds; a wrong move now would give the other a deadly advantage.

Herb broke the impasse. Reacting virtually on reflex, one hand flew to a strategically placed bakelite hand grenade while the other hand whipped the cap off it. Twisting his body, he threw the grenade violently at the German. The deadly ball struck the man and lodged near his chest. The panicked soldier gasped and wrenched his eyes from Herb. Frantically, he pushed himself up with one hand while he struggled to grasp at the harbinger of death with the other. While the German struggled, Herb dived under the lip of his trench, covering his head.

A bakelite hand grenade is triggered by movement. Once the

cap is released and the grenade is thrown, torque developed by spin allows an internal leaden weight to unwind a tape, which detonates it.

Herb waited for the blast. Why didn't the German shoot? Surely he must have time. It was the longest few seconds of his life.

The grenade exploded. The confined force lifted the Teutonic warrior a metre off the ground and turned him over. He landed on his back with a ghastly thud, right on the edge of Herb's pit. At the same time, the German's submachine gun spun off into space, slamming down next to Herb in his trench.

The eruption shocked Herb and covered him in dirt and smoke, causing him to splutter and gasp for breath. When he opened his eyes and sat up he froze; his blood went icy cold. The German's helmet had been blown off and his hair was plastered down, sticky with blood and sweat. His bright blue eyes were wide open and staring at him. At that moment, Herb couldn't tell whether the man was alive or dead.

Then he noticed the soldier's shattered chest and wretched blood-stained shirt. Herb tentatively prodded him. The man didn't move. He was indeed quite dead. Herb knew he would never forget those eyes. He would see them staring back at him forever.

He picked up the German's submachine gun, examined it and pulled the trigger. The firing pin clicked on an empty chamber. How strange: there were no bullets in it.

In the meantime, the other men in the section had similarly accounted for the remaining three soldiers. The immediate area directly in front of them was now saturated with dead Germans, their sweat-ridden bodies and grey uniforms caked with blood and dust.

The need for focus now sufficiently reinforced, Herb and his section kept stringent watch on the enemy over the next few hours as the sun waned. Now and then they would unleash a tirade at the enemy in an effort to relieve the pressure on the still contained D Company. Herb could see, with frustration, the remnants of the three platoons slowly being decimated.

In the meantime, on the left flank, B Company had experienced the same degree of attrition. Sergeant Wally Prior had assumed command and at 8.00 p.m., after fourteen hours of being pinned down in the fearful conditions and concerned about being completely surrounded, he gave the order for his men to withdraw. Fighting their way out and carrying their wounded with them, B Company had an effective strength of only fifteen men.

At the same time, D Company also began their withdrawal. Sadly, their numbers weren't any better: the other two sections of 17 Platoon, including Herb's old 4 Section, were virtually wiped out and the platoon was essentially leaderless. A private led the company out. In fact, at that moment, Herb, as acting corporal, was the highest ranking soldier in D Company, making him effectively company commander. Herb gave the retreating company covering fire and waited until it was dark.

At about this time, just as the light was fading, Herb noticed the Germans were also moving out; they appeared to be packing up. By 8.30 p.m., there was an eerie silence. He wanted to make sure that they had gone and said to his men, 'We're going to do a bayonet charge. I'll lead the first half of our section. If there are any Germans left there, I'm hoping they'll have had enough for today and I reckon they'll run.'

His men, like Herb, were exhausted, but they were prepared to follow Herb and finish it off. The first five men stood up, happy at least for the break from the cramped positions. With Herb leading, they gripped their rifles at the ready and raced towards the German positions.

No one shot at them. There was no one there; the area was

deserted. Tel el Eisa would belong to the 9th Division again. Herb's men left their protective piece of earth and began to move back. It was a great relief to leave this sickening place behind with its increasing stink of death.

For Herb's section it had been a successful day's work. Herb tallied that his section had killed at least 60 Germans and possibly wounded another 100 for the loss of only two men wounded.

As they walked past the two disabled British Valentine tanks which had been knocked out earlier, Herb kicked the outside and said, 'Come out.' The crew members slowly crawled out of the hatches, their hands held high in surrender, the darkness hiding the identity of the man issuing the command. Herb laughed and said, 'We're Aussies.' The relief was palpable. They walked back to headquarters together, all men laughing and grateful to be alive.

When the small troop arrived back at HQ, Lieutenant-Colonel Hammer interviewed Herb. 'What's going on out there?' he asked.

'I was nearly sure they were all getting out, sir. I could see them packing up and thought I'd help them out with a bayonet charge.'

'I want you to go back and have a look.'

'Yes, I will, sir, but with respect I won't take any of my men. They're exhausted.'

Hammer smiled. 'Hmm. No you won't. You've done enough. I'll send someone else. Good work.'

On his way out of the commander's tent, Herb was intercepted by the officer in charge of the British tank unit. He thanked Herb generously for helping to get his men out. In appreciation, he gave Herb a bottle of gin.

'Thank you, sir. I reckon this will go down well tonight.'

In the meantime, Lieutenant-Colonel Hammer released A Company from its defence duties and sent it, along with a platoon of 2/2nd machine-gunners and a troop of anti-tank guns, to investigate and occupy the German positions. They discovered that the Germans had indeed retreated. D and B companies had inflicted such serious casualties that they had been forced to withdraw. A Company occupied Tel el Eisa. The objectives of the battalion had been achieved.

In fact, it was one of only a few high marks for the Allied offensive that day. The 2/32nd Battalion captured Trig 22 on Makh Khad Ridge, but most other Australian battalions failed to gain their objectives, suffering heavy losses. Typical of the Australians' experience was the 2/23rd Battalion: in the past week, all company commanders had been killed along with 270 other casualties.

The valiant New Zealand division, which had attacked El Mrier to the south of Ruweisat Ridge, was beaten and overrun with severe losses. Worse was the devastating decimation of two British tank regiments which followed them into that same valley of death. Of 87 tanks sent into battle, only seven returned, with a loss of 150 men, all killed.

The 2/48th Battalion's victory also came at a high price. These tortuous and bloody slopes had claimed 53 men killed and 69 wounded. The day saw the most concentrated slaughter of men Herb had yet witnessed.

That night, even with the gin, sleep did not come easily to him. Alien feelings of depression washed over his shocked mind. He was reeling from the effects of his traumatic day. He battled to come to terms with the carnage he had witnessed. No training or previous insight had prepared him to cope with this degree of devastation. Where to begin?

The next morning, dawn crept in low and stealthy over the desert, revealing a scene of blood and thunder. Herb rose early and, with Padre Archbold, wandered over the battlefield, his mind numbed. There had been too much noise, too much tension and too much killing. The splendour of the full-frontal attack paled against this reality. The area was still reeking with the smell of burnt powder and death. He could not readily absorb the events he had survived. He quietly moved among the solemn burial parties searching for the wounded and burying the dead, enemy and Allied alike, his heart searching for answers.

In particular, he walked over the positions so gallantly held by his friends from 17 Platoon, in disbelief that they were all now either dead or wounded. Stan Gurney had already been interred; a rifle with its bayonet thrust into the dirt and a helmet on the butt marked the location of his grave. The burial party recorded finding a boomerang in his backpack, a reminder of his days back home.

He noted with some indignity that not all of the wounded Australians were afforded the same degree of mercy he himself had displayed to wounded Germans. Some had been finished off with a hole in the head. At least he was pleased to hear Lieutenant Jim Smith finally made it to safety after surviving fourteen miserable hours wounded in the hot sun.

For the following few nights, Herb wrestled uneasily with questions, difficult ones concerning life values and survival, haunted by grim visions of what he had seen. However, as much as he was affected by the attrition and grief, if he was to carry on with this war, as he had to, he knew he would have to put his deepest feelings on hold. Make sense of it all later. There was no stopping now; the enemy were still out there.

But putting aside his grief did not mean forgetting. Herb spoke to some of his friends who had fought beside him, and they all agreed Stan Gurney should be put up for an award. As only officers can recommend a decoration, Herb consulted the adjutant of the battalion. 'We'd like to put Gurney up for a VC, sir,' Herb said. 'I saw every bit of his action.'

'Well, it's unusual,' the adjutant replied, 'but seeing there are no officers left, and you, in effect, are the acting platoon commander and company commander, I'll approve and endorse the recommendation if you and two of the other privates would like to present it.'

'Thank you, sir, we'll do that.'

The July fighting wasn't finished quite yet. Auchinleck had one more desperate punch at Rommel. Both armies were groggy and running low on energy and resources, but on the 26th and 27th, he ordered a combined attack on Ruin Ridge, a feature of Miteiriya Ridge, by the 2/28th Battalion and by elements of two British divisions. The advance was met with an overwhelming barrage of mortar, artillery and anti-tank fire. On 28 July—one of the 9th Division's darkest days—most of the 2/28th Battalion was taken into captivity, losing more than 500 men.

It was the last major effort at this stage by both armies. The tragedy at Ruin Ridge brought the July offensive of the Eighth Army to a close. The first battle of El Alamein was over. Even though Auchinleck's forces had registered great losses, the one thing that mattered to the Allies was that Rommel had been halted. The Germans had also incurred great losses, and now both sides needed time to recover, re-form and build for an eventual decisive result.

Herb needed time also.

NINE

Prelude to El Alamein

As a result of the tremendous losses to the battalion in July, particularly after the brutal Tel el Eisa battle of the 22nd, a considerable amount of reorganisation was necessary. Lieutenant Peter Crompton was given temporary command of D Company. Until Crompton's arrival, for a few days Herb found he was the acting commander of both D Company and 17 Platoon, a rare responsibility for a private.

This lasted until Crompton appointed Lieutenant Murphy as platoon commander. He also appointed Bill Kibby, the platoon sergeant from Diver Derrick's 8 Platoon, as acting platoon sergeant of 17 Platoon. Herb had met Kibby before and liked him. He had been born in England and had come out to Australia at a young age, but was happy to be still called a 'Pom'. He had been a plasterer and decorator at Glenelg before the war and, now approaching 40 years of age, would be a steady and mature influence. He had already established a reputation for bravery and Herb knew Kibby would work well with him and the platoon.

Herb was installed as acting sergeant—a quick promotion—without really having served as corporal or section leader. This time, Herb accepted the rank without protest. He felt he was now up to the task. He was told he would also stay as leader of 5 Section.

On the night of 2 August, the 2/48th pulled out to Shammama Halt for a welcome rest in reserve. There, General Officer Commanding Lieutenant-General Morshead warmly congratulated the battalion on a job well done. He reinforced that their tremendous resolve and heavy sacrifice had put Rommel on the defensive. Importantly, he said, it had also helped destroy the German propaganda myth of Rommel's genius and invincibility. Like Mussolini before him, Rommel would have to reassess his initial ideas about conquering Egypt.

Shammama Halt was about a kilometre from the coast and, over the next few days, the men from the 2/48th relaxed and cleaned themselves up. While on the front line, there had been no real opportunity for maintaining cleanliness; Herb would splash some powder in essential places and occasionally 'take a bird bath' by dabbing himself with water. At Shammama they were completely resupplied with new clothes, particularly socks—it was important to keep feet dry otherwise toes would become diseased. (The old clothes were simply thrown away. They had became too rotten for resurrection.)

Interestingly, while resting, Herb became aware that while there were few other animals to be seen in the desert, birds of many varieties were plentiful. Day in, day out, thousands of ducks wheeled overhead, flying in perfect formation. Forced out of their nesting grounds by the shattering sounds of war, they often took to the beaches where they could be seen flying and circling. Inland, among the camel thorn and sagebrush, were quail, partridge and snipe. He also noticed that smaller birds often frequented campsites and fossicked for crumbs.

On the morning of 5 August, Herb decided he should attempt a swim for a wash, his first since his dip in the Sea of Galilee in June. As he was enjoying his splash in the Mediterranean, the news came through that the British prime minister, Winston Churchill, had just arrived at 9th Division's headquarters at Shammama.

Churchill had previously flown into Cairo on 3 August, primarily to lead conferences with General Auchinleck and other Middle East commanders. Besides discussing strategic policies, Churchill was concerned at the lack of immediate offensive action of the Eighth Army; the fight-back was not moving fast enough for him. He knew he would have to replace Auchinleck. Today, however, he would have a break and visit the troops.

Herb's mates insisted, 'Come on Herb. Churchill's driving around to talk to the boys. We should go over.' Herb was unimpressed. Like many others, he was still exhausted and needed his own time. 'Bugger Churchill. I'm having a bloody rest here.'

Churchill met with the Australian brigadiers and senior staff. He was most enthusiastic concerning the 9th Division's recent role, congratulating them for their part in 'stemming the tide' and telling them they had done magnificently. He then walked and mingled with the Australian troops, wearing a pith helmet and regularly giving his morale-boosting 'V for victory' sign. He also handed out a handful of his trademark cigars. (He was already well caricatured by the press as an irrepressible English bulldog defiantly resisting the enemy while smoking a cigar.) Later, one of Herb's mates excitedly produced a cigar for Herb to see when he came back from his swim.

The next day, Churchill determined that General Auchinleck be replaced. His first choice to lead the Eighth Army was a Tobruk veteran, Lieutenant-General William Gott. 'Strafer' Gott was a very experienced desert fighter, but was now tired and, of his own admission, uncreative as to how best to tackle Rommel. The appointment was never put to the test. While flying to Cairo the next day, Gott's Bristol bomber transport plane was intercepted and shot down by German fighter planes. Surviving the crash-landing, Gott was killed as he raced back into the burning plane to save those trapped inside.

Churchill then proposed to the British War Cabinet that Lieutenant-General Bernard Montgomery should command the Eighth Army. This decision would change the face of the war in the Middle East.

In the meantime, he placed General Sir Harold Alexander as overall commander of the Middle East Command. Alexander, a veteran of Dunkirk, was experienced and imperturbable. He arrived in Cairo on 8 August and quickly orientated himself to the situation. Montgomery arrived on the 12th and, on the same day, he and Alexander took afternoon tea in the luxurious lounge of the Ottoman-style Shepheard's Hotel, taking advantage of the cool breezes drifting in from the Nile which they overlooked.

Alexander issued only one order to the Eighth Army's new commander: 'Go down to the desert and defeat Rommel.' At 54, self-confident, voluble and unconventional, Montgomery was determined to do just that.

In the meantime, at El Alamein, while the land forces rested, the battle had shifted its main focus to the skies. There were always planes in the air, and the men of both armies were continually witness to dramatic overhead dogfights and see-sawing air battles, with crashing and burning planes an everyday occurrence.

A few days after Churchill's visit, Herb was having another dip in the ocean when he almost became a statistic of the air battle himself. In the skies above him, a German twin-engined Junkers 88C was involved in a life-and-death struggle with a squadron of Desert Air Force Hurricanes.

As usual, there were many planes in the sky and Herb and his fellow swimmers always kept a vigilant lookout for a renegade Messerschmitt 109 or a spontaneous bombing blitz from a rampant Stuka. The men were, after all, prime targets, sitting defenceless in the ocean.

The Junkers, a bomber, was weaving frantically to create a more difficult target for the Hurricanes, which were zipping around the plane like stinging gnats. The uneven contest couldn't last. Finally, one of the fighters unleashed a terrific fusillade that raked almost the entire length of the Junkers's fuselage. The bullets finished by smashing into one of the engines. Licks of orange flame darted and spat from the exhausts, escaping to form a trail of black smoke which quickly whipped into the slipstream.

The bullets also severed the controls of the rudder. That, and the loss of engine power, caused the plane to swing into a large circle, the pilot unable to control direction. Herb watched as the plane slowly arced over the sea, one wing dipping towards the ocean. As the spume of smoke grew thicker behind it, the plane quickly lost height and it appeared that it might actually crash right in the middle of the swimmers.

There were around 200 naked men splashing in the water with Herb, most generally enjoying themselves, but also keeping an eye on the entertainment above. Their mood abruptly changed. Helplessly, they visualised the plane's probable path. These bombers were known to carry a payload of 2000-kilogram bombs. If this one carried a full arsenal and exploded on impact, the concern was that the swimmers could be splattered like so many stunned mullets. Some men instinctively ducked under the water, others started racing for shore.

'My God Herb,' yelled one of Herb's mates. 'That Hun's been well and truly hit. It's coming pretty much right at us.'

Once again, Herb stood immobile, this time tethered to the sea bed and compelled by the vision of yet another German plane racing towards him. However, as before, the plane mercifully soared past him and the rest of the swimmers and pancaked into the water about 100 metres away. Herb braced expectantly.

The pilot, with a degree of skill and some luck, belly-landed the plane in a couple of metres of water. The rocketing vessel was accompanied by a brilliant spray of cascading water and a resounding crash. But thankfully, there was no explosion.

As Herb watched, the pilot and two crew members emerged from the damaged bird, then jumped. They landed in water up to their shoulders and seemed fairly unscathed. There was not one rifle or weapon among the Australians either in the sea or on the shore, but the naked men nevertheless closed around the airmen. The Germans, even through the tragedy of war and the seriousness of their position, could see the humorous side of their situation. They broke into smiles and put up their hands in surrender. The Australians responded spontaneously, laughing in return, and accepted the prisoners.

Over the coming weeks, to the troops, Montgomery appeared as a breath of fresh air. There was no doubt he was an experienced soldier. He joined the Royal Warwickshire Regiment in 1908 and was already a platoon commander by the outbreak of the Great War. During the war he was wounded twice and awarded a DSO (Distinguished Service Order). At the onset of this war, he was appointed commander of the 3rd Division sent to France.

Now, he quickly set about changing things. First, he issued orders that there would be no further retreat. Positive talk, at last. On 14 August, he visited the 9th Australian Division where he donned a 'digger' hat, which he would alternate with his black Tank Corps beret. He claimed affinity with the Australians as his father had been Bishop of Tasmania. To them, he exuded confidence, even cockiness, but it was what they needed.

'Monty', as he quickly became known, spoke only of attack. But his first task was to build morale. He declined to communicate through boring paperwork ('leave it to the staff') and made himself very recognisable and available. His philosophy was to show himself often and implant an image in the minds of his troops that he was energetic, realistic and capable. Although he often appeared prickly, his ruthless and unconventional demands—particularly for discipline—had an extraordinary effect on the men of the Eighth Army, building a revived hope and renewed confidence.

One important step was to concentrate both his tactical head-quarters and the Desert Air Force Headquarters close together. He worked with the commander of the Desert Air Force, Air Vice Marshal Sir Arthur Coningham. While building up his land army's fitness, resources and confidence, he insisted the air force keep Rommel off balance. He ordered massive air attacks over the lines of the Afrika Korps. It was vital that Rommel did not attack yet; Montgomery wanted to attack first and in his own time.

The air situation was distinctly changed from Tobruk. The Eighth Army's Air Force now enjoyed an advantage in the skies. All day, the Allied planes would fly over, eighteen at a time. The drone of Boston bombers would fill the air as they flew in close formation, dropping their deadly cargo in a grid pattern. As they flew back, they would be replaced by another team before reloading and returning to continue to block-bomb the enemy.

To cheers from the ground of 'There goes the football team again' (eighteen being the number of players in an Australian Rules football team), the deliberate and methodical bombard-ment was designed to steadily grind away at the enemy's confidence. In positive contrast to Tobruk, the unrelenting throbbing of the bombs empowered the men of the Eighth Army. As the days grew closer to the final onslaught, more bombers would come in as the army reserves built up. The planes protected a great army in the making.

* * *

In the first week of September, news came through that Stan Gurney had been awarded a posthumous Victoria Cross. This brought great excitement to the battalion, and particularly to the men of 17 Platoon.

'We should celebrate,' Herb said. 'Let's draw straws. The two longest go to Alex and buy beer.' As it happened, Herb and a mate 'lost' the draw and went AWL (absent without leave) to Alexandria. The two men stood on the roadside waiting to hitch a ride into town—about 70 kilometres away. Before long, an English major came along, driving a beat-up utility truck.

When the major pulled over, Herb related the story to him of why there were going to Alexandria. Thankfully, the major laughed, warming to the project; he thought it was a great story. With his pukka English accent, he told them to hop in the back of the utility, but advised them to take off their tan shoes. As Englishmen wear black shoes, and they would have to pass several provo (military police) checkpoints, the major thought it would be less complicated if they appeared as Englishmen.

The ruse worked. At Alexandria, the major waited for them while they bought their beer, then drove them back, right into 2/48th Battalion HQ. He roared off, laughing. And indeed, 17 Platoon had a suitable celebration for Stan Gurney, VC, well into the night.

The next day, the colonel called Herb to his office. Herb was concerned. He hoped he hadn't been found to have been AWL or that his platoon hadn't caused too much ruckus the previous evening. Instead, the colonel said, 'Your mates have put you up for a decoration for your leadership on 22 July. You've been awarded the DCM [Distinguished Conduct Medal]. Well done. Congratulations.' He smiled and extended his hand. 'By the way, you'll be interested, Wal Prior from B Company got one also for his work that day.'

Herb was dumbfounded: the DCM is the highest award for leadership; the VC is purely for valour. When he told his friends that their recommendation had been successful, they were just as excited for him as they had been for Stan.

'Let's go to Alex again and get some more grog,' they exhorted, prepared for another party.

However, Herb was disinclined to do this, somewhat overwhelmed by the 'gong' and the gesture. 'Thanks, fellas, but I don't think so. We've celebrated enough.' Clearly humbled, Herb was also still troubled by the trauma of that day. He had not come to terms with it yet.

At about this time, 17 Platoon received a new platoon commander, Lieutenant 'Tubby' Lewin. Lewin worked in well with Kibby and Herb, and his leadership helped the platoon prepare for Monty's promised fight-back. In the meantime, on the larger scene, reinforcements for the Eighth Army were steadily improving their position. Men had been shipped from Britain around the Cape of Good Hope to Cairo, then moved up to the desert. Equipment deficiencies were also being remedied. For the Australians, Crusader tanks, Vickers machine guns and 2-pounder anti-tank guns arrived (this time for the infantry battalions), while the 2/3rd Anti-Tank Regiment received 6-pounders, a much needed boost to their weaponry.

Meanwhile Rommel struggled to build up his reserves. His supply route from Italy to Tripoli in Libya was tenuous as aggressive Desert Air Force raids played havoc with German shipping. He was low on equipment, fuel and men. His troops were permanently hungry and suffering from all manner of illnesses. Morale was low.

The month of August was generally a quiet time during the day for the troops, but at night there was little respite. Aggressive patrolling by the Australians allowed them to dominate no-man's-land. Mainly, they needed to collect intelligence, so securing compliànt prisoners was high on their list of priorities.

Towards the end of August, Herb was pleased to meet the new D Company commander, Peter Robbins, the replacement for Major Williams who had been killed on that fateful 22 July. Herb liked him instantly. Robbins was of average height, had a fit physique and sported a crop of fair hair. He had a reputation for being tough but fair—a 'good' soldier. Herb would work well with him.

Shammama Halt was actually 30 kilometres from the front, and the role of the 2/48th at this stage was mainly one of defence against a possible enemy breakthrough. Reminiscent of Tobruk, the battalion was completely enclosed in a belt of wire and mines that formed a box. Things appeared peaceful enough.

The perceived quiet didn't last.

As August drew to a close, Rommel risked almost everything in one last throw of the dice when he unleashed a final effort to break through the Allied line. Fortunately, Montgomery had received intelligence that Rommel was about to launch his offensive. He knew that Rommel was about to commit his entire Panzer Army in a concentrated armoured assault to the south of El Alamein. Montgomery contrived to lure his rival into a trap.

Montgomery prepared strong defensive positions at the ridge of Alam Halfa, setting deadly minefields and positioning a force that included two tank divisions. There was soft sand here and, by cunning, he lured Rommel's force into this area. Misinformation left 'abandoned' in an Allied vehicle was found and taken as gospel by Rommel. He acted on it and was deceived.

On 30 August, Rommel ordered a diversionary infantry attack in the north while a force of 550 tanks and his best infantry supported by 3000 trucks attacked south of Alam Halfa. Monty's trap worked. The leading German tanks were caught in the minefields and soft sand. In reply, the British Eighth Army counterattacked with 300 tanks, several hundred anti-tank guns and 64 batteries of artillery.

At the same time, RAF Wellington bombers delivered the heaviest incessant bombing the Middle East had known. Over the next few days, Rommel's force was decimated. On 3 September, he broke off his assault and withdrew, his last immediate chance of reaching Cairo shattered. He had left behind hundreds of blackened, twisted vehicles and tanks, field pieces and guns, and 3000 men.

Now Montgomery would turn his attention to a full-scale offensive of his own.

On 23 September, the 2/48th Battalion moved back to Tel el Eisa, the same day that Rommel succumbed to a steadily debilitating and now chronic stomach and intestinal catarrh, and handed over command of the Panzer Army to General Stumme. Rommel flew out to Germany for specialist treatment.

Once again, aggressive patrolling for the men of the 2/48th was the order of the day. At night, sure-footed men would cross the gap between minefields searching for information. By now, the Germans and Italians had planted hundreds of thousands of mines in a great 8-kilometre wide belt spanning the entire 55-kilometre length of the El Alamein Line—the Devil's Garden.

Such was the enemy's realisation that the Eighth Army was gaining an overwhelming superiority in infantry, tanks, weaponry and command of the air, that they were forced to base their defence on a fortified line held by infantry. Their ability to carry out a mobile attacking role as they had done before was now limited.

By this stage—late September—Herb was feeling the effects of chronic dysentery. He could keep nothing in. A combination of stress, poor food and debilitating conditions was taking its toll. He was down to 9 stone (57 kilograms) and was very sick.

The battalion doctor transferred him to Alexandria for appropriate treatment.

In the meantime, British industrial effort and the gearing-up US war machine were pouring equipment, men and tanks daily into Egypt. Particularly prized were 300 new American Sherman tanks about to make their operational debut. There was great expectation they would be a match for the feared Panzers III and IV.

By mid-October, over 1000 tanks (of all types), 360 carriers and 8700 vehicles had landed at Cairo and were sent forward and over 1000 large guns were ready to cover the offensive. By contrast, the enemy had about 500 serviceable tanks ready for battle.

As well, four squadrons of Mitchell B-52 bombers boosted the Desert Air Force, and supplies and equipment of all sorts were stockpiled, ready for what could be only one purpose—a large-scale attack.

Broadly, Montgomery's plan was for simultaneous attacks to be staged in the north and south, with the decisive blow to be in the north—the Australian sector. By late October, Montgomery had organised the 220000 men of the Eighth Army into three groups: XXX Corps, XIII Corps and X Corps.

The Australians were part of XXX Corps, which contained a truly Commonwealth mix of five divisions made up of the 9th Australian, the 51st Highland, the 2nd New Zealand, the 1st South African, the 4th Indian and the British 23rd Armoured Brigade. The two other corps manned the lines further south and west, and consisted mainly of Free French, Greek and more armoured divisions.

Once the XXX Corps had punched two corridors in the Afrika Korps's defences, the armoured divisions of the X Corps would then break out. Part of the reasoning behind this plan was to fool the enemy into believing the main attack would come from further south. This entailed organising a massive deception. The construction of a dummy pipeline leading to the south was begun with the idea of misrepresenting not only the place of the attack, but the time. The work proceeded at a rate indicating it would not be finished until November, at least a fortnight after the actual planned attack.

Dummy guns, tanks and vehicles were constructed, disguising the actual movement of equipment. Every precaution was taken to maintain a normal-looking front to the enemy, as the scene was set for a deadly game of chess.

This deception was a remarkable feat considering the exposure presented by a bare, featureless desert and the regular daily surveillance and photography by German reconnaissance planes. By day, accompanied by huge clouds of dust, large movements of vehicles were deliberately seen to be headed south, leaving behind hessian and wood models of vehicles, tanks and dummy guns before returning north under cover of darkness, thereby creating the impression of a strong southern build-up.

By night the northern sector was stealthily strengthened, the evidence of which was kept hidden. Ammunition dumps were buried in the sand while gun pits, trenches and large weapons were camouflaged. The greatest concentration of the build-up was to be massed behind the 9th Division, opposite which the enemy's strength was known to be at its greatest.

Herb, recently returned from the hospital in Alexandria where he had celebrated his 21st birthday, was summoned together with the other company commanders on 16 October by Lieutenant-Colonel 'Tack' Hammer and advised that the large-scale attack they had been waiting for was about to commence. The object was primarily to destroy the 180 000 men under Rommel's command; merely containing them would not be enough. (Rommel's army consisted of four German and twelve Italian divisions.)

He broadly outlined the 2/48th's commitments for the

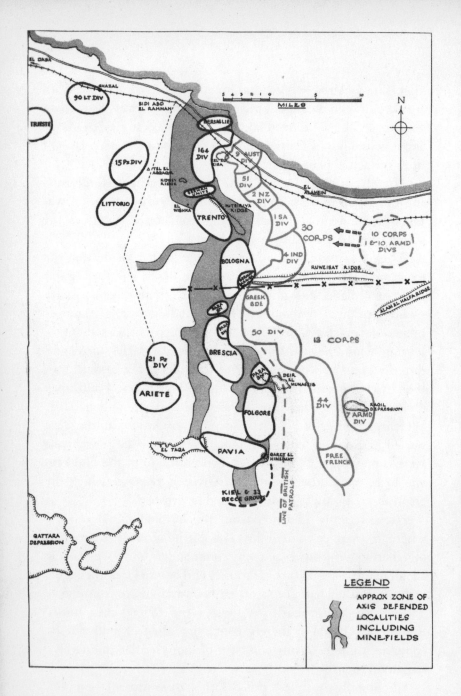

The Battle of El Alamein: Allied and Axis dispositions on 23 October 1942.

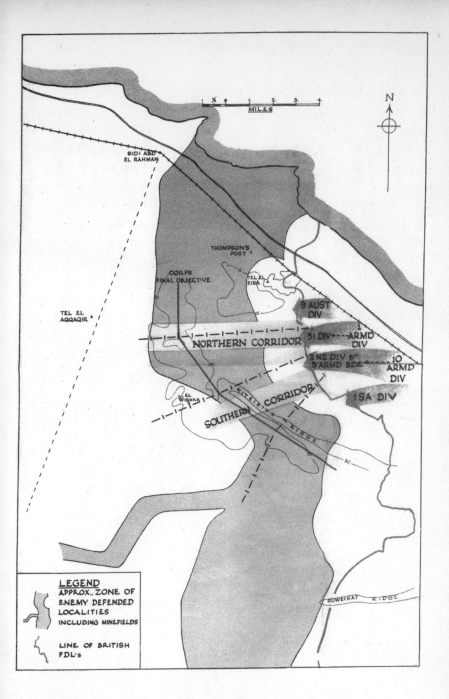

The Battle of El Alamein: the plan on XXX Corps Front.

opening parry and thrust. On the appointed night, the 2/48th's sister battalion, the 2/24th, were allocated the opening move. First, they would have to breach the minefields, subdue the opposing German incumbents (members of the hardened 164th German Infantry Division—a tough task) and advance 2 kilometres. The 2/48th were then to move through them and take the following 4 kilometres forward. As the 2/48th were placed in the northern-most section of the Alamein Line, their role was also to prevent Rommel outflanking the Allied forces in the 4000 metres between them and the sea. Their responsibility was critical.

On the evening of 22 October, the setting sun infused the rocky layers of the desert vaulting away to the horizon with incandescent crimson. At any other time, it would be pronounced beautiful. On this day, to the men of the Eighth Army, the colour was an ominous harbinger of the twelve days of blood-red battle that would follow.

PART III

El Alamein

TEN

The First Punch

Zero hour. 10.00 p.m., 23 October 1942.

For the second time in twenty minutes, Herb recoiled from the roar of the combined might of the Eighth Army's field guns, their omnipotence overwhelming. This time, the guns were concentrated specifically on the enemy manning the front line, softening them up for the assault to follow.

Strangely, over the whining of shells overhead, the crump of heavy bombs and cannon, and the clatter of machine guns, Herb became aware of another sound, incongruous at first, then, somehow, eerily suffusing the scene. An ancient call to battle, the high skirling wail of bagpipes set against the beat of drums filtered right across the battlefield, stirring the blood of all. The sound was created by the bandsmen of the 51st Highland Division, advancing well over to Herb's left. To Herb, in addition to the primal response, the music imbued a strange sense of connection and security triggered by Australia's traditional Scottish colonial ties. The Highland Division had only recently arrived in the desert in August although, due to many joint training programs, many solid friendships between Scots and Australians had already been formed.

Herb watched as, right across the battlefield, line upon line of steel-helmeted figures with rifles at the high port, bayonets catching in the moonlight, plugged at a regular 75 paces per minute towards the enemy positions.

The pace rate was critical. In the generally featureless desert, objectives were difficult to recognise, particularly at night. Rehearsals and training ensured every soldier would move at a uniform pace so that they would arrive at a certain point in co-ordination with artillery coverage. Once they had reached their objective at the programmed time, the pace would change. The artillery fire would then move at a rate of 100 paces every three minutes.

To Herb's immediate left, the 9th Division's 20th Brigade began their advance, while to his right the 24th Brigade created a separate diversion in order to draw the enemy's attention northwards. Right along the line, men in other units also moved towards their objectives: in the south, the XXX Corps divisions—New Zealanders, South Africans and Scots—targeted Kidney and Miteiriya ridges; further south, the armoured (tank) divisions tried to penetrate the minefield; and, just ahead, Herb watched intently as the men from his sister battalion, the 2/24th—now almost shrouded in dust and smoke—plodded towards the enemy's lines.

Following a continuous overhead stream of coloured tracer shells directing them towards their target, they disappeared from Herb's view into the blackness. A few moments later, emanating from this abyss, Herb was aware of an escalation in the intensity of small arms fire, signalling that the battle was engaged. Enemy shelling joined the din and mingled with indiscriminate yells and commands, all of which filtered in a confused and eerie fashion back through the darkness.

A strong smell of cordite drifted over the battlefield and caused Herb's eyes to smart. Blearily, he peered through the darkness and haze, searching for signs that the 2/24th had reached the enemy's front line. Suddenly, the success signal went up. A Verey flare exploded into the sky. The 2/24th was at the enemy's first line of defence and was about to fight towards its next objective. Now it would be Herb's turn.

At 12.38 a.m., the command was given to the men of the 2/48th, 'On your feet. We're going in!' Herb's D Company, under Captain Peter Robbins, led from the right, while B Company moved out on the left. The other two companies, A and C, followed in reserve. At once, the tightness in Herb's stomach relaxed as imagination and fear were replaced by action and substance. In fact, to his surprise he felt a strong sense of excitement as he acknowledged he was caught up in the centre of a significant and epic drama. However, this adrenalin buzz was tempered by the knowledge that at any second he could just as quickly be dead.

Movement was not always easy; everyone carried extra ammunition and some men shouldered heavy sheets of corrugated iron to be used later for protection. Since the opening bombardment, except for five minutes' break just before 10.00 p.m., the massive rapid-artillery battery fire had never ceased. Arousal was always high, prompted by consistent noise, explosions and flashing lights. The sky was continually bright.

Within moments, the battalion came up against the enemy's second line of defence. These positions were heavily wired, mined and booby-trapped. However, with the assistance of skilled sappers they were quickly dismantled and breeched. But no sooner had they broken through the line than the battalion came under intense crossfire from isolated pockets of enemy resistance. Herb's 17 Platoon went to ground, bullets from enemy rifles and machine guns whizzing around them. Within seconds, the platoon commander, Lieutenant 'Tubby' Lewin, was hit in the knee. Other men yelled as they too were hit.

Sergeant Kibby searched for Herb, upon finding him saying, 'Herb, Tubby's been hit and so have a couple of others. I've called for the medico to get them out. I'm in charge. You're now platoon sergeant. Captain Robbins just found me and wants our platoon to get rid of that troublesome post holding up the company's advance. Can you hold things together here while I go and see what the problem is?' It was a statement more than a question. Before Herb could respond he finished with, 'Follow me when you can.' Herb saw Kibby disappear into the darkness, then immediately set to work checking on the whereabouts of the remaining platoon members. Within minutes he had assembled and prepared them for a charge behind Kibby.

Kibby was equipped with a Thompson submachine gun, in combination with which he was known to be particularly lethal. Through the darkness, about 50 metres away, Herb heard the unmistakable sound of the Tommy gun's chatter, ripping in bursts through the night. Screams filtered back through the air then, suddenly, everything was silent. A few minutes later, Kibby appeared, silhouetted in the moonlight, and walking behind about eight square-helmeted Germans with their hands high in the air. As he got closer, he smiled. 'Fixed that,' he said. 'Got a few of the blighters. The rest of them gave up. I'll send these chaps back.'

Herb nodded, silently impressed. His reputation was indeed well earned; independence, audacity and courage were obvious hallmarks of Kibby.

There were still a few pockets of Germans in the immediate vicinity and, for the next hour or so, the platoon fought to clear the way. The going was tough. Generally, the battlefield logistics were confusing. Rifle fire, machine guns, mortars, flashing and exploding lights, sudden darkness, smoke and dust, powerful artillery explosions, were all set against a background of muffled yells, commands and orders which echoed from every corner of the front. 'Take that point there!' 'Shut that mob up over there!' 'Knock off that machine gun!' Cries from the wounded and dying added to the disorder.

Inspired by Kibby's example, the men from 17 Platoon quickly responded to the challenge. As sergeant, Herb kept the men moving, cajoling and motivating each section leader in turn. As they walked past the gun pit that Kibby had cleared earlier, Herb counted eight dead Germans, collapsed in various poses of death. What devastation.

As part of his responsibilities, Herb moved around the platoon ensuring each section had ample ammunition and supplies, and checking on the wellbeing of individuals. Intermittently, he came under fire himself and would have to shoot himself clear. But always leading from the front was Kibby, setting the pace and standard for the platoon.

In this manner, the battalion worked as a well-oiled machine, relentlessly overrunning all mortar, machine-gun posts and anti-tank guns. At 3.45 a.m., Lieutenant-Colonel Hammer instructed that the battalion send up its success signal, almost 4 kilometres on from the original start line. Fortunately, the battalion had relatively few casualties with four killed, despite taking 70 prisoners and inflicting heavy loss of life on the enemy. Out of the four divisions, the 2/48th Battalion was the only one to dig in where planned. On their immediate left, the 2/13th Battalion from 20th Brigade encountered fierce opposition and were slowed until tanks arrived to assist them. This prevented them linking up with the 2/48th at the correct time and place.

Without the 2/13th's flanking protection, the 2/48th had effectively cut a deep wedge in the enemy's line and now had two fronts to protect. D Company were set up to face north, while C and A faced the open west and northwest flanks. They realised they could probably expect a strong counterattack from the enemy at first light. Herb settled himself into a pit, crouching underneath a half-sheet of galvanised iron, and waited.

Behind them, through the path they had just cleared in the minefield, followed vehicles carrying mortars, Vickers machine guns and other supplies. Engineers placed a protective double row of 2400 Hawkins mines around the 2/48th's position. These were simply tin-can mines and were placed on the ground—a kind of mobile minefield. By dawn, the battalion was ready to fight again.

Meanwhile, the Highlander, New Zealand and South African divisions had succeeded in gaining some, but not all of their objectives. In the southern sector, the armoured divisions were held back in their advance by a lethal minefield, the taped lanes which had been set up to guide vehicles through the minefields becoming bottlenecks with lines of traffic up to 3 kilometres in length. Others, fearful of being caught in the open as the morning light strengthened, hid behind wadis, ridges and wrecked vehicles. At the end of the first night of battle, the Eighth Army had not accomplished what its commander had ordered, yet the foundations were nevertheless solidly set for victory.

Well before dawn, Herb could hear the clanking, roaring and squealing of enemy tanks immediately in front of the battalion's positions. He waited for sunrise, expecting a strong counter-attack. However, as the early morning sun lit the horizon, planes from the Desert Air Force streaked out of the grey darkness, flashes of sunlight sparkling off their wings. They banked, then screamed into the attack, dropping a hail of bombs on the growling tanks. Through the cordite and dust haze, Herb could make out black smoke curling from the burning and wrecked colossi. There would be no attack from that quarter this morning.

In fact, there was no counterattack on the 2/48th at all that day—from tanks or infantry. But the Afrika Korps artillery and mortars had recovered and released a sustained heavy fire on the battalion. Throughout the day, the artillery of both armies pounded opposing positions right along the line.

The Australian 20th Brigade wasn't as fortunate as the 2/48th. The 2/13th and 2/17th battalions desperately fought off aggressive Panzer attacks all day, with the 2/13th losing their commanding officer late in the afternoon. But they were resolute and immovable. By dusk, more than 30 Panzer tanks lay smouldering and destroyed in front of their positions, as well as a few new American Shermans.

During the day, in the XXX Corps sector, the High Command was becoming increasingly concerned about another matter—the extreme accuracy of the German guns. It soon became obvious that the bombardment was directed by observers situated on a rise known as Trig 29, about 1.5 kilometres from the 2/48th's forward companies. The feature, about 7 metres higher than the surrounding countryside, commanded a clear view of the brigade's positions and the immediate area to the south. It was vital ground. And would become more so as the battle wore on.

That morning, as the heat built up, Herb sweltered under his corrugated iron hatch, but it was safer than being outside. The artillery offensive continued all day, regularly crashing sand and rocks on to his shelter. From his hutch he also witnessed many air battles as the Desert Air Force strafed and bombed enemy positions and tangled with enemy fighter planes. In fact, that day, planes from the Desert Air Force flew more than 1000 sorties.

There had been some humour earlier as, during an intense escalation of fire, one Italian officer decided he'd had enough. Wearing only his white underpants, he brazenly walked over to the 2/48th lines and enquired, 'Are prisoners welcome?' On being told they were, he returned to his lines and brought out four other Italians.

The early morning also saw the loss of the Afrika Korps commanding officer, General Stumme. Stumme was well aware that the early artillery bombardment and the following offensive were on a scale unheard of since the last year of the Great War.

So fierce was its effect that confusion and panic made organisation difficult. Communication lines had also been shredded, although Panzer Army headquarters was receiving some broken information. In the north, they heard that Allied infantry had broken into the main defence line across a front of 10 kilometres and, in the south, an attack of about 100 tanks had overrun the outpost but had been stopped in front of the main defence line.

Stumme decided to assess the position for himself. Accompanied by a driver and a colonel, he planned to go as far forward as the German 90th Light Division. However, he missed them and drove right up to the front, careering into the midst of the Australians. Rifles and machine-gun fire riddled the car. The colonel was killed immediately, shot through the head, while the driver violently swung the vehicle around and roared off at full speed. Meanwhile, General Stumme suffered a fatal heart attack and fell out of the vehicle, dying alone in the desert.

Leaderless, the enemy was clearly at an immediate loss to organise a strong counterattack, one which the Allies could have expected if Rommel was at the helm.

Most of the Allied land action on this day, the 24th, centred on the southern sector as tanks from the armoured corps tried to bridge the minefields. In return, the enemy mounted attack after attack throughout the day, but although tanks and lorried infantry were flung in lavishly, all enemy assaults along the front were broken up. The encounters left at least seventeen German tanks shattered and destroyed. However, it was obvious that the intended initial Allied breakthrough had stalled.

Even though the men of the 2/48th received a welcome hot meal that night, Herb found there wasn't much opportunity for sleep. He was acutely aware that just a few kilometres south of him, the 2/13th and 2/17th battalions of the 20th Brigade were involved in a desperate fight for their positions. However, by morning they had reached their objectives. All battalions were now on line.

As daylight of the 25th quickly revealed, the tactical key to the security of the campaign was going to be the ownership of Trig 29. Its value was that from it one could see 4–5 kilometres in every direction, including the railway line to the north and a great deal of XXX Corps's area to the south. It had to be taken.

Meanwhile, Montgomery had realised that the failure of the initial southern breakthrough necessitated a switch in plans; he decided to attack now on the northern flank, using the Australian 9th Division as the spearhead. XIII Corps, in the south, was to go entirely on the defensive. Overall, he reasoned, the change in tactics would also keep the enemy guessing.

Montgomery called for plans to be made for an attack on Trig 29. Australian commander Lieutenant-General Morshead chose the 26th Brigade. The 2/24th and 2/48th battalions would do the job. Later that afternoon, Lieutenant-Colonel Hammer received written orders to take the feature and the spur surrounding it. Trig 29 sloped east for about a kilometre and finished at an area known as the Fig Garden, or Fig Orchard. The 2/24th would take the Fig Garden.

Before Hammer called a conference of his commanders, fortune played a lucky hand for him. In the fading light of the day, an enemy patrol of two German armoured cars and a lone Panzer ventured close to the battalion's front line. They were spotted by a platoon of Vickers machine-gunners from the 2/2nd Machine Gun Battalion. Crouched behind their Vickers, they allowed the German party to approach to within 100 metres, then observed them where they halted. The Germans relaxed, hands on hips, and listened to the subdued talk and laughter coming from the men of the 2/48th Battalion conversing during their evening meal.

The Vickers shattered the relative evening quiet, startling both enemy and friends. Diver Derrick's 8 Platoon joined in from the 2/48th. Five Germans fell dead and three were wounded, one calling out 'Kamerad'. There would be no more response. Several men brought in the survivors—two German officers and two senior NCOs. The senior officer happened to be the colonel commanding the 125th Infantry Regiment of the 164th German Division, the group holding the northern sector of the front opposite them. The junior officer was the acting commander of one of the battalions of that regiment.

It was a good haul. Both were carrying marked maps and sketches showing the enemy's dispositions around Trig 29. Some of the men from the 2/48th were from the Barossa Valley in South Australia—a well-known wine-producing area with strong German ancestry and tradition—and spoke and understood German. Through these interpreters, the younger officer confirmed to Hammer that the track running to Trig 29 was not mined. This would allow Hammer to create a built-in surprise for the defenders during the planned assault.

Meanwhile, at dusk Field Marshal Rommel had returned to the desert in his favourite plane, a Storch, ready to resume his command. The Afrika Korps was in crisis, and his organisational and leadership skills were about to be tested as never before.

Later that evening, Herb, along with the officers and NCOs of the 2/48th, was briefed on the coming attack. As they were squatting around a rudimentary dugout, an enemy shell exploded about 10 metres away. Shrapnel whistled through the air and everyone spreadeagled on the floor. No one was hurt, but Herb noticed most of the men were now strategically reclined as Hammer, unperturbed, continued to relay his plans.

'It's our responsibility to capture Trig 29 and the spur around it. Tonight.' Hammer pointed to the map showing the position of Trig 29. The feature was about 1.5 kilometres from the 2/48th.

'Part of the plan is to form a mobile company using the battalion Bren carriers. These will carry some of us straight to the top. We've just found out that the positions on the track leading to the spur are unmined, courtesy of some prisoners just brought in, so hopefully we will surprise them by driving right up to the high point.

'The plan is this. As we move off we will be covered by a large artillery blanket, which will continue to blast the point while we advance. Two forward companies, D and A, will move to 900 yards [about a kilometre], halt and protect the flanks. C Company, mounted on ten carriers charging four abreast, will then ride in to within 200 yards [about 220 metres] from Trig 29, then jump to the ground. They will arrive there exactly three minutes after the artillery shelling stops, then they will take the point. Precision will be paramount. We'll have some anti-tank guns towed behind some other Bren carriers in the wake of C Company in case we get some tanks thrown at us. Some Vickers machine-gunners will also march in with them, as well as the mortar platoon.

'As soon as we get going, the 2/24th will form up in our just vacated area. Their objective will be the Fig Garden, east of Trig 29, and they will eventually try and take Thompson's Post, further north. We also know from the prisoners that Trig 29 has just been reinforced and is heavily armed. They will be determined. We move at midnight. Good luck.'

ELEVEN

Trig 29

From Herb's position, Trig 29 looked like a large sand dune erupting out of an otherwise featureless desert. Sunday 25 October was the day after the full moon, and by midnight the moon was high above the horizon, throwing a shimmering white reflection over the desert and highlighting the objective ahead. Herb was nervous, but he hoped the moon's glow would work to their advantage.

Since 10.00 p.m., there had been a heavy background noise of artillery and mortar fire as, further south, the 1st South African Division initiated a diversionary bombardment in that sector. Above the noise, Herb could hear a squadron of Wellington bombers approaching his direction, and right on midnight they dropped 115 tons of bombs onto Trig 29. At the same instant, 250 guns from the 9th Division artillery units and other regiments plastered the protruding feature with over 15 000 rounds, an inordinate amount of firepower for one target.

The explosions illuminated the sky for kilometres in all directions; the prominence of Trig 29 was clearly silhouetted against the orange and white flames. Thick dark smoke swirled into the blackness, twisting up into the night sky. The scene was sinister and Herb almost felt sorry for the enemy hiding from the fury. Trig 29 was taking a pounding.

Realistically, though, Herb knew that in a few moments' time he would be there himself; the more damage inflicted now, the less he would have to cope with later. The start line for the men of the 2/48th was a 100-metre-long white tape stapled into the sand. At exactly the same instant as the first bombs crashed on the target ahead, the battalion moved off from the start line. Herb's D Company marched out on the right side of the track, A Company on the left.

A Bofors gun fired coloured tracers above the track to lead the way and direct them. The Bofors was a Swedish-designed anti-aircraft gun, requiring a crew of eight to run it efficiently, and it was set up directly behind them. However, they had only moved a few metres when the enemy countered with massive artillery and mortar attacks. Dust, smoke and noise from crashing and exploding shells suffused the area.

The battalion trudged on, but 400 metres from their start point D Company went to ground, pinned down by machine-gun fire as well as artillery. Captain Robbins called out, 'There's a Jerry post up ahead. Everybody down.' Bullets cracked and whined, splitting the night air and kicking up dust where they bit into the sand.

Bill Kibby took the initiative once again. 'You're in charge Herb. I'll be back in a few minutes.' He disappeared into the darkness.

Lofty Whaite, now recovered from his earlier stress disorders, called to Herb. 'Where's the Sarge going? Shouldn't he take a section along?' (A section is eleven men.) Herb shrugged his shoulders.

Within another minute, Herb heard the chatter of Kibby's Tommy gun rattling above the sound of the Spandau and background artillery fire. The Spandau stopped firing. Yells were heard. Peering into the murky darkness, Herb could make out five or six dark figures in square helmets emerging towards them, hands held high. Kibby was walking behind, his Tommy gun aimed at the Germans.

'Path's clear again,' he smiled.

On the left flank, A Company had also come under heavy fire. They were taking losses, but were able to continue on to their first objective.

Meanwhile, the Bren carriers, with the men of C Company walking behind, were following closely, waiting for the success signal that A and D companies had secured their first objectives.

The carriers were commanded by Captain Zac Isaksson. Isaksson's first concern, before he had access to the German prisoners' recent information, was the possibility of encountering minefields along the way. To guard against this, he had ordered sandbags to be placed under the base of each carrier in an effort to limit casualties.

The carriers, known as Universal Bren gun carriers, were driven by powerful Ford V8 engines and moved on tracks. They had a Bren gun mounted in front and were lightly armoured, but were not well protected against machine guns. They also had an open roof, which left the crew of three—the commander, driver and gunner—and their cargo, vulnerable to mortar attack. Weighing just over 4 tons, they were generally utilised more like tracked jeeps than mini-tanks.

On the right of the carriers, now that Kibby had cleared the machine-gun post, D Company was able to move forward again. However, all three platoons, 16, 17 and 18, continued to encounter strong resistance. Communication often became difficult between platoons and headquarters as the artillery bombardment regularly cut the connecting cables. Three times, Kibby ventured over open ground into the night. Following the damaged cable, he would trace it through to locate the shattered ends and effect repairs, often attracting attention and fire.

Herb was often under fire himself. As well as maintaining

cohesion with his three platoon sections, he would have to fight his way through entrenched German outposts. Two of his men were wounded during this period, and such were the hostilities that the other two platoons, 16 and 18, lost their commanding officers. Captain Robbins became the only remaining officer of D Company. Eventually, the company reached the success point, having taken 38 prisoners on the way.

The success signal from both A and D companies—a Verey gun—was fired and further back the troops from C Company clambered aboard the Bren carriers, six men to a carrier. At the same time, the artillery stepped up their rate of fire, heralding the final dash of the carriers and C Company to the Trig.

This extra noise also served to blanket the throaty roar of the powerful V8s and the clanking of the tracks as the ten carriers relentlessly charged at 15 miles per hour (27 km/h) towards the peak. They covered the remaining kilometre in nine minutes and, in perfectly synchronised timing, arrived exactly one minute after the artillery barrage lifted.

The original plan was for the carriers to stop about 200 metres short of the trigger point. However, due to the covering noise of the artillery, the speed of their approach and the smoke and dust on the Trig, Isaksson and the commanding officer of C Company, Captain Mick Bryant, decided to drive almost to the top. Their arrival was a complete surprise to the enemy.

As the carriers ground to a halt, virtually right in front of the entrenched Germans, the troops jumped out. At once, they became engaged in a fierce firefight. Isaksson swung the carriers around then waited to see whether they could assist. After a time, they returned back down the spur, passing through A and D companies. Meanwhile, Herb and D Company continued to fight their way towards the Trig on the right, while A Company proceeded on the left. Both companies ran into the most hideous opposition, mortars and machine guns splattering the desert.

A Company became pinned down. Verey guns lit up the scene and gun flashes highlighted and revealed individual positions. The pressure was relentless. The commander of 7 Platoon, Lieutenant Taggert, and four of his men were killed in rapid succession, shot from a burst from a Spandau 50 metres ahead. Other men fell wounded; the platoon was being whittled away. The company commander, Bob Shillaker, contemplated withdrawing a little to try another flank.

However, such was the resolve and calibre of these men that this option wasn't necessary. Forty-year-old Percy Gratwick, one of only seven remaining men from 7 Platoon, sprang from his position. With a grenade at the ready in his right hand and his rifle in his left, he dashed into the lethal fire. Herb knew Gratwick, but not well; they had both arrived at Tobruk in the same intake the previous year. All he really knew about him was that he had been a tough gold prospector from Western Australia.

And, it would appear, he was fearless. Sprinting like an athlete, Gratwick narrowed the distance to the mortar and machine-gun post. At 20 metres, a German submachine gunner opened up and bullets sprayed all round, whistling through the air. Miraculously, none hit him. Gratwick hurled the grenade, watching it explode among the mortar crew behind the gunner. He dropped to one knee and threw another grenade. It burst not far from the first, sending fragments to all corners of the post. Screams echoed back.

Jumping to his feet again, bullets still humming all around him, Gratwick charged into the gun pit. Giving no quarter, he bayoneted the gunner then killed all the remaining members of the mortar crew before destroying the mortar itself. An instant later, he was shot down and killed by other machine guns.

Not stopping for pause, Captain Shillaker seized the moment, and the other men followed. Gratwick's splendid and gallant charge had changed the tactical situation, unsettling the enemy and inspiring his companions. A Company took the advantage and charged at the surprised enemy who were reeling from the effects of Gratwick's selfless effort. Several machine-gun nests, however, continued to spew murderous crossfire at the Australians.

Eight Platoon commander Diver Derrick also rose to the challenge. Commandeering one of the returning Bren carriers, he sprang into it and stood in the centre of the vehicle. Standing defiantly, his upper body exposed and gripping his Tommy gun, he directed the driver to roar back into the battle. Several of the German machine guns swung and fired at him, spreading a broadside of flame across the battlefield. The bullets rattled off the carrier, pock-marking the metal sides and clattering like hail on a corrugated iron roof. Incredibly, none hit Derrick or the driver.

A stray bullet ignited a Verey cartridge in the back of the carrier, the resultant flash lighting up the scene and capturing a rampant Derrick, grinning like a Cheshire cat. As he charged into the hail of fire, to his troops it was an indelible image of a resolute warrior risking all. Gaze narrowed and focused on the machine-gun pits ahead, Derrick pressed the trigger of his own submachine gun and sprayed burst after deadly burst at the enemy. Others in his unit yelled to each other in disbelief. 'God, he'll never come out of that. He's gone. We won't see Diver again.'

The carrier thundered through the cauldron, driving right up to each of the three gun pits. Derrick annihilated each one in turn. Maintaining his determined grin, he ordered the driver to back up to each position and checked that all had been silenced. The path was now clear. Shillaker signalled to the company and, steadily, it continued to work its way towards the Trig and C Company ahead.

In the meantime, D Company was also under tremendous fire on the right flank of the spur. Robbins, without his platoon commanders, continued to lead by example. He was everywhere, supporting and prodding. In 17 Platoon Kibby did the same, directing fire and encouraging his men. Twice more he ventured into the darkness to repair broken communication cables, each time dealing with any enemy who dared venture too close. The three platoons slugged it out, metre by metre, steadily moving towards C Company, who were by now well engaged in their own mortal struggle.

Earlier, when C Company sprang out of the carriers virtually on the Trig itself, they became immediately immersed in a vicious hand-to-hand battle, the intensity of which had never before been experienced by the battalion. The cream of the German 125th Panzer Grenadier Regiment was solidly entrenched in these positions, and was giving no quarter.

Machine-gun nests, mortar instalments and rows of entrenched German infantrymen fought back with the ferocity of cornered tigers. As light flashed from bomb bursts, frozen effigies of desperate men locked in deadly combat reflected the primal struggle. Men fought on sand and shale, clawing for an advantage, bayonets flashing in the moonlight.

The Australians were skilled and second to none in cold-steel conflict. Eventually, by about 2.00 a.m., the Germans on Trig 29 had been beaten. From his position on the right flank, Herb could see the Germans retreating off the Trig. By the time the success signal was fired, the enemy had lost more than 100 men taken prisoner, and nearly as many killed.

While the three companies worked at consolidating their positions around Trig 29, Colonel Hammer ordered that the loaded supply trucks of B Company, waiting 550 metres behind the original starting point, move up to the Trig. At that moment, disaster struck.

An Italian artillery shell landed among the trucks, igniting one laden with mines and explosives. An ear-splitting explosion lit up the sky, emitting a wall of flame that silhouetted every man and vehicle for metres around. In turn the flames triggered detonations in seven more trucks all carrying mines. The resultant series of eruptions created a roar accompanied by a tremendous shock wave. The effect reverberated clear across the immediate battlefield. The concussion was so powerful, the driver of a vehicle 100 metres away was thrown from his truck.

Herb felt the ground vibrate and saw the inferno from his position on Trig 29, feeling vulnerable and exposed even at that distance. He suppressed a desire to dig deep into the shale and hide; abject fear always simmering just below the surface. 'My God,' he uttered in disbelief, 'that looks like our supply trucks. No one will get out of that alive.'

Angry curls of yellow and black smoke whirled into the dark ether as the ghastly screams of men being burnt alive echoed over the desert. Men on fire threw themselves onto the sand, writhing in agony as they tried to quench the flames. Stretcher-bearers raced into the burning wrecks, one emerging with an injured man on his shoulders. A cheer went up from the astounded onlookers, but they were silenced as the rescuer was blinded by the fire and staggered into another burning truck, only to die an agonising death. Ten men died as their vehicles were blown to pieces; none got out. Other men were incinerated as they raced in to help.

The intensity of the explosions attracted the attention of the German artillery who proceeded to concentrate their fire on the blazing area, inadvertently taking some pressure off the three companies on Trig 29. The bombardment destroyed other nearby trucks and killed an ambulance crew. The carnage resembled a scene from hell that would have stretched even Dante's imagination.

The other effect from this devastation was the loss of 2000 mines and all equipment required for B and D companies. They were completely destroyed. The push for Trig 29 could be compromised. Reacting to the tragedy, one man, Major Tucker, responded by organising five other trucks to return to the supply dump to ferry the necessary equipment, mines and ammunition forward. He was assisted in this by Captain Isaksson who had reorganised his Bren carriers and maintained a shuttle service. For the next few hours, his carriers, as well as the trucks, raced to and from the starting line to a new supply dump not far from Battalion Headquarters, about 500 metres south of the Trig. On the return trips they would carry the wounded, most of the journeys made while under heavy and continuous artillery fire.

In the meantime, the 2/24th Battalion had set off on its assault of the Fig Garden at 12.40 a.m. As with the 2/48th, they encountered very heavy enemy resistance. Eventually, however, they reached and took their objective. They then moved towards their second objective, Thompson's Post, a little further north. Here, they were subjected to intense fire from enemy posts on the flanks and, shortly afterwards, were forced to withdraw to the Fig Garden. At the Fig Garden they linked up with elements of the 2/48th Battalion, creating a salient from Trig 29 across to the Fig Garden and then curving in a crescent between Trig 29 and the 2/15th and 2/17th battalions on the left. That night, the other sectors of New Zealand and South African divisions occupied the whole of the Miteiriya Ridge.

As the morning light revealed the situation, Rommel observed the 2/24th and 2/48th battalions consolidating their positions. By dawn, the 2/48th had laid 2400 mines in front of their positions and the troops were entrenched, corrugated iron firmly covering their heads. Rommel was furious. It had been reported to him that there were 30 tanks on Trig 29. (His informers had obviously mistaken the smaller carriers for tanks.)

Rommel had lost two of his battalions, completely destroyed, and, as the men on Trig 29 now found, he had lost a position of pivotal importance. As the morning light intensified, the extended field of observation for the Eighth Army became clear; the position would be invaluable. Rommel reacted vigorously. He gave orders that every available tank, gun and man be thrown into the task of recapturing Trig 29.

The men of the 2/48th Battalion were exhausted. That night, with the 2/24th, they had lost 55 men killed and 256 wounded. It had been a night of action, drudgery and attrition, but every member had reason to be satisfied. They had bloodied Rommel's nose. But they knew there would be little rest. Surely Rommel would counterattack with a vengeance.

TWELVE

Consolidation

Before dawn on the morning of 26 October, Herb could hear the ominous rumbling of enemy tanks, rolling into position somewhere in the darkness in front of him. It was a frightening and menacing sound; he still had fresh memories of his recent and painful experience when one had tried to grind him into the dirt at Tel el Eisa.

At first light, he counted some 30 tanks milling directly in front of Trig 29, then watched them line up about a kilometre away in preparation for battle.

However, the enemy artillery had the first punch. With the dawn, the men on Trig 29 were greeted with one of the most punishing bombardments they had yet endured. 'Here it comes,' yelled Herb. 'Get under cover.' Herb squeezed into his shallow pit and braced himself. Within minutes, the mound was choked with dust. Hundreds of shells shrieked across the sky, before crashing down on the Trig. Fountains of earth and rocks erupted in a fiery cauldron, spraying dirt and sand in all directions. Herb hid deeper under his corrugated iron shelter, praying he didn't receive a direct hit. It was a massive invasion of soul, mind and body.

The barrage continued until 9.00 a.m., answered in turn by the 9th Division's artillery. Morshead had at his disposal fire power from four Australian artillery regiments and some

English and South African 25-pounders and larger guns. The artillery duel continued for most of the day.

As the morning heat built up, Herb sweltered in his protective cocoon. Was it only a few hours ago that he was sympathetic to his enemy on the same worthless piece of ground? Things were about to get hotter.

Some German helmets were seen bobbing towards his position. Rommel had sent in 300 infantry to move in support of the tanks. The infantry were only about 500 metres away, and Herb was certain they would attempt an open-field attack. If they did, it would be near suicidal—a measure of Rommel's desperation. Herb checked his rifle and waited.

That same morning, Rommel had, in fact, moved his 21st Panzer (tanks) from 40 kilometres south to the northern-most sector, although the ones opposing Herb now were from 15th Panzer. Rommel's decision was an irrevocable gamble; he knew that if it didn't pay off he would not have enough fuel to allow the tanks to return south. However, if he was to stop Montgomery he must beat him now, in the north. In addition he called forward his army reserve, the tough 90th Light Division with its lorried infantry, mobile artillery and machine guns.

In the meantime, that same morning, Montgomery realised his early push had virtually stalled. The most ground had been made by the Australians, who had penetrated almost all of the 8-kilometre minefield and were now pushing northwest towards the coast. When he received information Rommel was moving his tanks and troops north, he decided to switch his main effort 8 kilometres further south. This point was opposite the critical juncture between the German and Italian forces; a perceived weak link.

At 11.30 a.m., Montgomery called in the commanders of all three corps to a conference in Lieutenant-General Morshead's dugout headquarters. He informed them that for the next few days, the Australians would continue their attacks in the north. The operation would begin on the evening of 28 October.

Morshead had no sooner left the meeting when, just after lunch, the 300 enemy troops and tanks in front of Herb gave signs they were intending to advance. It was to be the first of 25 attacks over the next two days. Immediately, Allied heavy artillery and mortars opened up on the combined force. Several tanks burst into flames as the bombardment shredded the area, and troops hit the ground, trying to escape flying shrapnel and rocks.

As soon as the barrage lifted, Kittyhawks screamed across the sky. Flying low over Herb, their blue exhausts illuminated the wings and the 250-pound bombs hugged the fuselage. As one, they rained their bombs on the German tanks. Several Panzers exploded in roaring balls of fire; others were rendered impotent by flying shrapnel, their tracks ripped apart and their guns silenced. The planes then circled around to commence strafing runs.

The Kittyhawks hurled their defiance at the enemy as they roared over the battlefield, strafing both the tanks and the lines of troops. The devastation and terror were complete. Men reeled under the impact of the bullets and more tanks were left upturned and in flames, ribbons of black smoke spiralling upwards.

As a result of both the artillery attack and the Kittyhawk sortie, the area had become a cauldron of smoke and flames. The smell of smoke, cordite and seared flesh hung over the battle-ground. Dead men littered the field and hulks of shattered tanks bearing the palm and lightning-forked swastika insignia of the Afrika Korps were left derelict. Herb could see groups of men limping and running back to their own territory, cowed by the ferocity of the attack.

There were several more attacks on the 2/48th that day, most of which were repelled by intensive gunfire. Tanks, trucks, and German and Italian infantry tried to breach the forward companies' defences, but were each time turned back. Once, a squadron of Stukas unleashed their shrieking bombs on the Trig. The Stukas were terrifying and dangerous, but didn't stay around for long; the air was now dominated by the Desert Air Force, as many as three to one. Worst, however, was the 88-mm airburst which swept the battlefields. These were deadly and intimidating, lashing everything mercilessly and spewing cruelty wherever they exploded.

Squadrons of Allied bombers flew all day, concentrating on particular targets. As well, the artillery bombardment right along the line rarely stopped. Late in the afternoon, more noise came from the area of Kidney Ridge; a large tank battle resulted in the British being forced back. After four days and nights of continuous racket and confusion Herb and his troops were becoming seriously sleep deprived, yet every effort was made to stay alert as it was critical for survival.

It was obvious the Australian 9th Division had become the centre point of the battle. Not only was the 20th Brigade under attack but the 26th Brigade, further south, had also been subjected to heavy fire. The growing body count only reinforced this. On 26 October, the 2/48th Battalion lost 62 men killed, wounded or missing; more than in all the previous days of the battle combined. The enemy also suffered heavily this day, losing 116 tanks, all destroyed.

The pattern of this level of fighting continued, increasing in intensity as Rommel applied even more pressure to regain the Trig. For both armies, 27 October was a day of desperation— particularly so for the defenders, the 20th and 26th brigades. It began with a strong German infantry and tank attack on the 2/24th Battalion at 4.00 a.m. and continued along the line against all battalions as the long day progressed. Every man of the 2/48th felt the sting as tanks, artillery, infantry and bombers seethed around this hotly contested square kilometre of earth.

The strongest penetration so far was delivered at 4.00 p.m. Herb noticed a squadron of enemy troop carriers drive up to within 2 kilometres of the Trig. They were halted there by immediate fire from the artillery, but 30 minutes later a battalion of infantry formed up and commenced advancing towards the 2/48th.

The 2/48th responded with open slather. Artillery together with mortars, machine guns and rifles opened up, and a wall of searching fire cut into the enemy ranks, decimating the charging men. Herb supported his rifle on the sand mound in front of his pit and rapidly fired round after round. Supporting the infantry attack, German artillery increased the heavy shelling of Trig 29 and used smoke shells in an attempt to blind the observation posts. At one stage, the smoke and dust on the Trig became so congested that Lieutenant-Colonel Hammer ordered the mortars and artillery to cease fire as the machine gunners couldn't see the enemy.

As the Panzer grenadiers and infantry out in front of Herb's positions were recovering from the assault and others were groggily getting to their feet and trying to re-form, they became caught in the withering fire from the powerful Vickers machine guns from a platoon of the 2/2nd MG Battalion attached to the 2/48th. Artillery concentration hit the Germans also and temporarily forced their withdrawal.

However, by 5.00 p.m., another large attack developed—the largest that day. The battalion was attacked from two sides: armoured cars, tanks and infantry approached from the north and northeast. Attackers and defenders began firing simultaneously. The pressure was relentless as exhausted men from both armies fought through a blistering hail of bullets. But such was the determination and intensity of the 2/48th resistance that the Germans got no nearer than 300 metres. They retired to dugout positions about 600 metres away and regrouped.

It was obvious to Herb that the Germans had taken heavy casualties. He could hear cries for help—terrible cries of dying and wounded men echoing back from the battlefield area. In fact, the enemy lost 80 killed and 200 wounded in that attack.

At this stage, Morshead had planned for the 2/24th and 2/48th battalions to be relieved by the 2/17th Battalion for 24 hours in order to prepare for the major offensive to be launched on the night of the 28th. It was a welcome measure.

At about 11.00 p.m., Herb and 17 Platoon gratefully extricated themselves and began to move into a safe rear position. They were desperately looking forward to a long-awaited sleep. A series of Verey flares exploded into the night sky just as Herb was passing the incoming forward troops of the 2/17th. The flash revealed a large contingent of Germans approaching and massing a few hundred metres from the Trig.

One of the 2/17th men said to Herb, 'Where's the enemy?'

'Well,' Herb answered, dragging a smile to his face, 'if you look out there, you'll see the bastards lining up, waiting to have a go at us, ready to attack. We're leaving.' Herb chuckled. 'See you later.' Both men laughed. The situation was serious, but humour, black as it was, always seemed to help.

Herb had only left the soldier for a few moments when yelling and gunfire signalled that the German attack had commenced. Captain Robbins ordered D Company back to the fighting area. 'It's another large-scale attack. We've been called to help.'

All companies of the 2/48th were dispatched to reinforce the 2/17th. Both battalions linked in a blistering stand-up firefight. Peering into the darkness through the dim light of the rising moon and then under the glare of the searching flares, the enemy became clearly visible.

The artillery opened up and the infantry threw every available weapon at the Germans—Vickers, Brens, Tommy guns, rifles and mortars. Flames and bullets saturated the enemy positions for about 45 minutes. Then all was silent. Steadily, cries of the wounded broke the silence and filtered back to Herb. The enemy had been held to within 150 metres of the Australian line, and some were lying just in front of the perimeter. Herb could hear trucks revving from the enemy's quarters and then screeching to a halt. Then he heard them driving into the darkness. Yet again, the Australians had proved their commitment to holding the Trig.

Once it was obvious the German attack had failed, the 2/48th resumed moving off the Trig. By 3.30 a.m. on 28 October, the battalion was resting in a secluded area south of Tel el Eisa. Here, Herb dug a shallow trench and, after a welcome hot meal, sunk into a deep sleep, the first real rest he had enjoyed in five days. He was exhausted, filthy and hollow-eyed, yet he savoured the sense of triumph which pervaded the battalion.

Over these five days they had created two successful attacks and had thrown back many advances initiated by the Germans. All the while, they had been under intensive fire themselves. Sleep was precious; Herb knew he would be out there again tonight. And it would probably be harder this time as the battalion's fighting strength was now reduced to 415 men (from an original 696 on 23 October).

In fact, serious casualties were mounting for the Eighth Army, and particularly for XXX Corps. At this stage, the 9th Division had suffered 1668 casualties, although the Scots, who were still fighting for their objectives, had incurred more with 1956. However, Rommel had lost far more men, tanks, artillery and planes, and he was in a position where he could far less afford to. This was Montgomery's 'crumbling' operation—a gradual wearing-down process.

The other major concern to Montgomery was that the Australian Government was agitating for the recall of the

9th Division because of the local Japanese threat. Morshead was aware of the government's request to Churchill and, on the morning of 27 October, had requested a meeting with the commander-in-chief, General Alexander, at Montgomery's tactical headquarters. Neither Alexander nor Montgomery had been informed of the Australian Government's decision, but Alexander said that he could not possibly consider releasing them: without the Australians, the battle would collapse.

Tomorrow would be another day.

THIRTEEN
Pushing North

The next morning, 28 October, Lieutenant-Colonel Hammer called a meeting of his company commanders and outlined the plan for that night's attack. It was a daring plan, and complicated. Basically, five battalions from the 9th Division were to thrust north and northeast, using Trig 29 as a pivot point. The idea was to capture the railway line and main road in an effort to cut off Rommel's supply route and to negate a large number of the enemy forces.

During the first phase, the 2/48th Battalion would be in reserve while the 2/13th and 2/15th battalions undertook the initial 2-kilometre penetration. The 2/48th's sister battalion, the 2/23rd, would then attempt to reach the railway line and main road. The 2/48th would follow by attacking east along the main road to Ring Contour 25, while the other sister battalion, the 2/24th, would attempt to take Thompson's Post again. This would all happen before sunrise.

That afternoon, Captain Robbins relayed the plan to his platoon commanders and NCOs. Herb was immediately concerned. The 2/48th commitment was reliant on the 2/23rd fulfilling their objective on time, and the 2/23rd had a difficult assignment.

The 2/23rd were to begin their battle by moving through the minefields, mounted on 40 tanks. When they had achieved this, the 2/48th would then move through the 2/23rd and continue on to take Ring Contour 25—all before sunrise. It was very ambitious—even for men who were fresh, which they weren't. Importantly, nobody wanted to be caught out in the desert in daylight; it would be certain murder.

Herb was nervous again. So were his platoon members. The 9th Division had been asked to perform a great deal. Herb and Bill Kibby spent time talking the plan through with their troop. Herb considered that, generally, morale and confidence were high; however, fatigue and the enormity of the task were challenging them. They distracted themselves by cleaning their weapons and preparing their equipment and ammunition. Herb had selected a Thompson submachine gun for this fight. He meticulously oiled and cleaned it, wanting it to respond perfectly. He then spent silent time contemplating the coming battle.

At 7.30 p.m., in the fading light, the battalion moved out in lorries to a position near Trig 29. No one spoke. At 10.00 p.m., they were ready. They had been directed to wait in the trucks until they received a success signal from the 2/23rd Battalion, who were now still milling around the assembly area. The 2/24th were also waiting with them for the same signal.

Meanwhile, the tanks from 46th Royal Tank Regiment arrived at 10.30 p.m., bringing immediate and unwanted enemy attention to the assembly area. While the 2/23rd men were climbing aboard the tanks, heavy German shell fire caused some casualties. At 11.18 p.m., with pennants fluttering in the now chill night breeze, the tanks with their human cargo aboard crossed the start line. Herb watched them rumble into the night, silently urging them to be quick.

Specially equipped tanks known as Scorpions led the troops onto the battlefield. Herb was intrigued. The tanks had two steel arms which projected well forward, on which was mounted a rotating shaft. The shaft was driven by an auxiliary engine fitted to the tank, and short lengths of heavy chain attached to the shaft flailed the ground, exploding any mines a few metres ahead of the tank. One great disadvantage, however, was the large cloud of dust raised which obscured the vision of the tanks following behind.

Immediately, four tanks were disabled by mines as they strayed off course. Some tanks became helpless, blocking the path of others following, and some of these reversed onto more concealed mines. Pandemonium was fast developing. Enemy anti-tank guns fired mercilessly at close range, their brilliant tracer-streaked shells quickly finding targets. Some that didn't pierce the armour whined and ricocheted off into space amid a shower of rainbow sparks. Further difficulties with communication and navigation compounded these problems. Herb and the men from the 2/48th could see and hear that the battle was not going well.

Burning tanks filled the night with a ghastly light. 'My God, there's another one going up.' They could hear the build-up of small-arms fire as the 2/23rd infantry dismounted from the tanks and began to chase after enemy machine-gun and mortar emplacements. All the while, German flares pierced the sky, throwing surreal shadows and visions over the scene, distorting and magnifying the terrifying images.

Waiting for battle can often be as disturbing as actually taking part. Obsessive thoughts are allowed to replay—'These could be my last moments on earth'. Action, on the other hand, pushes speculation into the background. As the long hours drew on, some of Herb's men paced up and down, while some tried dozing in the trucks but couldn't. Stray enemy shells often whizzed past nearby. One made a direct hit on a truck, killing a man; another truck exploded, wounding seven more. As the battle intensified and the hours crept on, nervous men dug holes and hid from the increasing artillery attack; 88-mm guns added to the tension by firing airburst shrapnel. One exploded directly over 16 Platoon, killing one of Herb's friends, George Adcock.

It eventually became obvious that the 2/23rd was in serious

trouble. The soldiers of the battalion had advanced about 600 metres into German territory and were under heavy fire. They had sustained about 200 casualties, many of them being brought back past the 2/48th positions. Most of the Royal Tank Regiment tanks had been destroyed; only seven remained and they had withdrawn to the perimeter to give support, if required, against a possible enemy counterattack at dawn.

By 4.00 a.m., it became obvious to the commanders that it would be senseless to send in the 2/48th. The operation would be postponed. After waiting for an intense six hours, with a profound sense of relief the 2/48th Battalion was transported back to the Tel el Eisa area. The exhausted men fell into their pits to sleep just as dawn was breaking.

Herb and his men relished the chance for a 'breather'. As the morning warmed up the next day, heat and flies prevented satisfactory sleep, but that night, the battalion was able to grab six hours of vital regenerating slumber.

Before turning in for the night, Captain Robbins sought out Herb and asked for a private word. Robbins, like everybody, was very aware of the intensity of the situation. He was also acutely aware of his own mortality.

'Herb, if something happens to me, I want you to recommend Bill Kibby for a DCM. Since he's taken over as platoon commander, he's been a tower of strength. I want you to particularly mention his achievements on the 25th when he fixed the signal cables five times.'

Herb agreed. Like Robbins, he had become very much a realist. Both men knew that at any moment, in a battle of this magnitude with this degree of attrition, either of them could be killed instantly. There was little place for the romantic notion that they alone would be spared.

During that day, 29 October, the overall tactical situation had changed. Incredibly, the 2/23rd Battalion, diminished to 60 men, had been able to turn their seemingly hopeless situation into a victory. The other 9th Division battalions had also managed to hold their ground, but with similarly great losses.

Meanwhile, Rommel had lost two complete Italian battalions. He was feeling the effects of Montgomery's unrelenting pressure. By dawn of the 29th, he had decided that if his losses became too great he would have to withdraw 80 kilometres. Montgomery, on the other hand, continued with his plan to launch a breakout operation. It was to be a decisive attack, code-named Operation Supercharge, and would be launched on the night of 31 October and led by the New Zealand division across the Rahman Track. However, he still needed the Australians to maintain their crumbling action in the north; they would commence their attack on the night of 30 October. There would be a heavy price for this decision: it would be the most costly and bitter fighting ever encountered by the 2/48th Battalion.

FOURTEEN

Precursor to Operation Supercharge

The day of 30 October started badly. Herb was resting fitfully, grateful for the break from hostilities, when in the early hours of the morning 30 Stukas streaked out of the western sky. They dived vertically, machine guns blazing, spitting at targets around the perimeter. At the bottom of their dive, before straightening out, they released their aerial bombs. Fortunately, no real damage was done, but an hour later, after breakfast, nature had her turn. A notorious desert *khamsin* rose like a giant thunderhead, throwing tons of sand hundreds of metres into the air.

The sand trembled there precariously, like the crest of a wild surf wave, then crashed, sprawling and seething over both armies. For a while, the grains of desert sand and dirt blocked out the scarred scene of inhumane carnage, half-burying the dead and the living alike. Herb struggled for air as he covered his face with his shirt and searched for a dust-free corner of his trench where he could breathe. The discomfort continued for most of the day.

Under the storm's cover, Lieutenant-Colonel Hammer discussed with Brigade Headquarters the details of the coming night's attack. Eventually, on dusk, the *khamsin* abated and an eerie silence prevailed. It would not last. Hammer, on his return from Brigade Headquarters, outlined his plans for that night's operation. He told his company commanders that although their task had been amended from the original, it was nevertheless an ambitious request. As well as having to capture Ring Contour 25, they had also been given the extra objective of turning north and taking the position known as Cloverleaf. Their phase of the operation would begin once 2/32nd Battalion had secured the area around the main road and railway line at a place called the Blockhouse.

Over the last eight days, the 2/48th Battalion had been steadily depleted. The total strength of the rifle companies was down to 213, averaging less than eighteen per platoon. Everybody knew they had a difficult assignment.

Just after nightfall, Herb and Bill Kibby once more directed their platoon members onto the back of a lorry. It was the fourth time in eight days that they would face the enemy. The battalion was driven about 2 kilometres north of Trig 29 to the communal assembly area, which contained men from all four battalions, milling about and preparing to walk through the gates of hell once more.

At 10.00 p.m., assisted by an accompanying artillery barrage, the 2/32nd moved off. They had scarcely melded into the gloom when the 2/48th formed up on the same start line. By 10.30 p.m., they too had left. In their wake, a further ten minutes behind, the 2/24th followed, and close on their heels at 11.00 p.m., the 2/3rd Pioneer Battalion too set off.

The general movement was north towards a feature called Barrel Hill, about 3 kilometres away. It was the 2/32nd's task to capture and secure the hill to allow the following battalions to break off and attack their separate targets.

Barrel Hill, also known as B11, was a small feature only 11 metres high which sloped gradually, rising towards the southeast. It was the only noticeable feature in a largely flat landscape, and gave command of the road and the railway line. From its

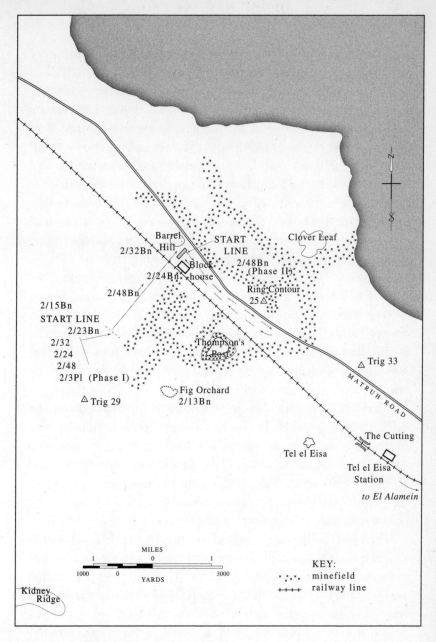

2/48th Battalion action, 30–31 October, El Alamein

crest, which was flat-topped with a curling lip, a troop of strongly entrenched enemy held the position.

Almost immediately, all battalions came under heavy fire, the 2/48th receiving a vicious crossfire from both flanks. Lieutenant-Colonel Hammer ordered the advance companies C and B to clear the way. Herb's D Company was close behind and he could hear the escalating fire in front of him and to the sides. Now and then, he would take a quick shot in the dark at some distinctive flame from an enemy rifle. He was never sure if his bullets found their mark, but the overall firepower allowed the battalion to steadily make ground. Even though they suffered a few casualties, they reached the railway line within an hour.

However, conditions in this region were far from stable. The 2/32nd had not yet completely fulfilled their objective, having battled under the most intensive fire. Barrel Hill was still in enemy hands, as was the railway line and the Blockhouse. The 2/48th Battalion's planned start line for phase two was about 400 metres beyond the railway line and roughly the same distance again before the Blockhouse.

Herb could see that crossing the railway line was going to be difficult and potentially deadly. Enemy tanks, mortars and machine guns were set up on a series of ridges, most giving direct coverage of the railway line. Spandaus, some entrenched on Barrel Hill, enfiladed it incessantly. Hammer sent a group of men from Intelligence Section to cross the railway line and to lay the start line in preparation for phase two.

However, these men quickly came under fire. Hammer called for support and all companies pressed into the attack. The railway line was in a cutting about 4 metres deep. The men realised that the instant the Spandaus stopped firing, there was a few seconds' breather before they commenced again. In this break, the men from the 2/48th scrambled down the embankment and raced over the railway line, Herb bracing himself and sprinting across just as the firing started again. It was like a game of Russian roulette.

Bullets thudded into the dirt, while others ricocheted off the metal lines, showering sparks and whining off into the blackness. Herb rolled under the other embankment, spitting sand from his mouth. He didn't rest long. Germans were embedded in trenches right across this feature. Ahead of him, men from B Company had been dropping grenades into the Germans' pits, then blasting the soldiers inside with their rifles. Herb and 17 Platoon followed and did the same. It was close, dangerous work, but effective. It was also nasty. Watching a man being blown to pieces at close range was ugly.

By the time he had reached the new start point, he had run out of grenades, but the position was theirs. Now the battalion had to wait for the artillery barrage to herald the next phase. They were due to move east down the road with the 2/24th Battalion moving parallel to them on their right. Their first objective was Ring Contour 25, about 3 kilometres away. They would then turn left and capture Cloverleaf; the 2/24th were to turn right and take Thompson's Post.

While waiting for the artillery barrage, Hammer moved the battalion into a depression about 150 metres forward of the start line; the men called it the Saucer. He considered this would lessen the risk of being hit by enemy artillery fire. Unfortunately, they also came under some 'friendly' fire from their own 25-pounder guns. Quickly, casualties mounted. D Company's new lieutenant of 16 Platoon, Terry Farrell, was the first to be hit. Another shell landed with a thud in the centre of D Company. Herb instinctively burrowed into the ground, trying desperately to get away. Cold fear gripped him, but mercifully the bomb round didn't explode on impact. The relief was palpable, but the waiting was getting on everybody's nerves. Then, at 1.00 a.m. the battalion was called to line up.

At this stage, an Australian soldier wandered out of the darkness and approached Herb. He introduced himself as Nowac. He asked Herb, 'Who are you?'

'We're the 48th.'

'You'll do me. I'm absolutely lost. I'm from the 32nd. I was cut off just as they were going in to attack. They're copping hell over there. I'm not a deserter. I just can't find them. Can I go with you?'

'Sure,' said Herb. 'We'll need all the help we can get, I suspect. Come along. We're just about to move off.'

The plan was for the artillery barrage to begin at 1.00 a.m. and then to move 1 kilometre ahead of the advancing battalions. This gap amounted to about fifteen minutes. It was worrying. Considering the enemy's strength, Hammer realised it would give the Germans too much time to regroup after the barrage had passed them. They would be waiting for the 2/48th as they advanced.

Hammer urged his men to get closer to the protective barrage. With due caution, the battalion moved steadily along the main road on a front about 350 metres across. The strategy appeared to work for a while. The forward scouts noticed the enemy in front get up and race to ground further back. They didn't fire on them. In fact, they encountered very little resistance at all, until they rounded a small bend, a dog's leg to the left. Ring Contour 25 was about 40 metres ahead. Then they were hit by everything. The men they'd pushed back were now waiting in ambush. Herb realised it was too late. They should have fired on them earlier.

Verey flares lit the scene. Bullets from machine guns and rifles spun through the air, and mortars and larger artillery pockmarked the territory. Men fell quickly, killed or wounded. There was nowhere to go. The two leading companies, B and C, quickly lost officers and men. A Company moved up to re-inforce the line, also quickly losing its officers.

Herb and D Company swung off to the north, dangerously close to a minefield, while withering fire continued to slice through them.

The battalion had come up against Rommel's experienced 125th Regiment from the 164th Light Division. During periods when the sky was lit, Herb could make out two mounds directly in front of them, joined by a saddle. The damage to his company was being inflicted by a raking and murderous fire spitting from these mounds.

Within seconds, D Company was out of contact with Battalion Headquarters; all members of D Company Headquarters, including the signallers, were subjected to the vicious crossfire. Men fell like dominoes, most killed, some wounded. Herb could hear the yells and realised there would be no more communication with Hammer. They were on their own. Over to his left, he saw the commander of 18 Platoon, Lieutenant Treloar, fall, his leg smashed by machine-gun bullets. The 16 Platoon commander, Lieutenant Farrell, had already been evacuated. Once again, Captain Robbins was the only remaining officer in D Company.

Robbins called for the remaining men in his command to go to ground. It was pitch black as he was trying to regroup his men. Herb heard a machine-gun rattle not far from Robbins's position. He knew from the sound it was the hated Spandau. The cadence of it was embedded in Herb's memory since Tobruk when one had almost finished him. Herb heard cries from one of his men, 'Get Kibby.' Then, closer, a muffled choking sound.

A flare illuminated the scene. Suddenly, Robbins emerged out of the darkness and appeared burnished, standing in front of Herb. He opened his mouth as if to speak, then Herb noticed he had both his hands clasped around his neck. He was trying to prevent precious blood from seeping out of a gaping wound. He staggered a little, startling Herb, who moved forward to support him. Robbins moved his hands away from his neck to reveal his wounds. But it was too late. He sank to his knees then dropped, his body draping over a barbed-wire entanglement, his life gone. Herb was rocked; he stood motionless for a second, trying to contemplate the loss.

Robbins was a man he had greatly admired, both as a soldier and as an individual. And he was gone, just like that. He felt anger welling deep inside. This war was already very personal. How many more friends and good men would he have to lose?

Another burst from the Spandau. Herb ducked. Nearby, 'Chuck' Fowler, a close friend of Robbins, fell instantly.

Bill Kibby appeared alongside Herb. Sighting the fallen Robbins, he registered what had happened and immediately took charge.

Although the company was scattered and had gone to ground, he gathered the remnants together. He could muster about a dozen men—the rest were out of action, either killed or wounded. He ordered Herb and a section of men, which included Len Steicke, Tom Martin and others, to take one mound; he would take the other. Herb didn't like the idea of Kibby going by himself—it wasn't sound military logic—but Kibby was used to working alone.

In the meantime, the other three companies were still under heavy fire, experiencing the same attrition rate as D Company. As key officers and brave men fell, their deeds often unrecorded, other men stood up to take their roles and responsibilities.

The commander of A Company, Captain Shillaker, was badly wounded, leaving Sergeant Diver Derrick in charge. The C Company commander, Captain Bryant, amalgamated the depleted A and C companies, now numbering only 45 men. B Company quickly lost most of their officers, and Battalion Headquarters, which had moved forward, was also under heavy fire. The assault was furious and shocking. Men were falling, being attacked from the rear as well as the front; the area was becoming a living hell. It was now about 3.00 a.m., and Hammer decided that, because time was running short and manpower was so seriously depleted, he would not be able to take the Ring Contour 25 position. The best he could do was to hold the road in front of it.

By now, Herb's section of men had advanced to within 20 metres of the Ring Contour. He could hear the Germans yelling to each other. Tremendous gunfire was being traded between both groups. The machine-gun fire from the Germans was particularly vicious. During bursts of light from artillery fire and Verey pistols, Herb saw his men defiantly standing their ground and then steadfastly advancing through the tirade. His friend Lofty Whaite was over to his left, repeatedly aiming and firing his rifle. Ray Bloffwich, the Bren gunner, aimed his weapon from the hip, sending a burning cavalcade of bullets at the enemy while 'Blondie' Gwynne, not far over from him, was doing the same with his .303 rifle. Len Diddy, the other remaining sergeant of the company, who was now commander of 16 Platoon, took up the right flank. Herb's mate Norm Leaney was there while other men filled the gaps, all solely intent on the left mound of Ring Contour 25.

Grenades from both groups thumped in Herb's ears, mixing with the short snap of rifles, the deep-throated chatter from his own Tommy gun and the sharp bursts from the Bren gun. The tenacious section of men gained several metres; they were doing some damage. Screams echoed back from the mound, but soon it became obvious that the weight of numbers was too much. Herb looked in dismay as one by one his men were cut down. One of the first to fall was Nowac, the 'recruit' from the 2/32nd, dying bravely as he stood with Herb's men.

Herb's good friend Lofty Whaite was also caught in the fusillade, falling wounded beside Nowac. Ray Bloffwich, the Bren gunner, also dropped, Spandau machine-gun bullets riddling his body. Remarkably, he could still crawl and began to extricate himself from the battlefield.

Len Diddy, the 16 Platoon sergeant, collapsed, receiving a bullet. Steicke and Martin also fell, the sweep of the Reaper's scythe unrelenting. This was the deadliest place Herb had ever been in. Desperate thoughts flashed through his mind. How could anyone survive?

However, against these odds, his small section of men steadily continued to make ground. Remarkably, the pressure of their attack was beginning to tell. He could see Germans falling, some running back as his now handful of men advanced. Herb kept firing his Tommy gun in small bursts, quickly emptying his circular magazine. The magazine held 50 .45 bullets; the gun even now reminding him of gangsters and Al Capone. Herb whipped off the spent magazine, threw it away and reached into his side pouch. Grabbing a vertical magazine, which held twenty bullets, he clicked it into place.

More men fell beside him. 'Blondie' Gwynne was knocked off his feet by a solid sweep of machine-gun fire, shattering his rifle. He lay on the ground, stunned.

Meanwhile, over to the right, Bill Kibby was carrying out a one-man vendetta. There are times when fear drops beyond the threshold of the mind, relegated far into the background. These are moments of great exaltation, of tremendous physical exertion, when action dominates all that is cerebral, overcoming fear. As with the knights of old, Kibby was engaging his deepest instincts. This is the face of battle, up close, stark and menacing, allowing an individual to remain responsible for his soul, yet not necessarily master of his fate.

Kibby charged towards the enemy post, throwing hand grenades one after the other at the entrenched machine-gunners. The deep explosions contrasted with the sharpness of the gunfire. Men screamed. Suddenly there was silence. Kibby had destroyed the post. There was a lull in the gunfire and he started to move over to Herb.

Herb had heard the action and seen the explosions. As usual, the smell of cordite was strong in the air. Smoke and dust clouded his vision, but then Kibby appeared, moving out of the murky darkness. He got to within a few metres of Herb, and Herb turned sideways to talk to him, narrowing his profile. The move saved his life. In the eerie light reflected from the battle-ground pyrotechnics, Herb realised Kibby was about to say something. Then the dreaded sound of a Spandau cut the air. Five bullets ripped through the front pouch of Herb's webbing, ripping it to shreds. The thud stopped Herb in his tracks. More bullets whizzed close to him, then shrieked out into space. Then one smashed into Kibby's neck. To Herb's horror, he saw the bullet enter the front of his throat, pierce his jugular vein then explode through the back of his head. Blood spurted over Herb's shirt and webbing.

Kibby instinctively grabbed at his throat. Words tried to form, but all that came out was a sickening gurgle. He dropped at Herb's feet, his blood trickling into the parched desert sand. There was nothing Herb could do for Kibby. His training and experience under fire triggered him into action. He would need to be decisive; he would have to take command of the company.

There were still machine gunners out there. He turned and yelled a command in the dark. 'Right fellows. Follow me. We're going in.'

Blood pumping, he charged towards the direction where he had seen the spitting flame. Fifteen large strides powered him to the edge of the German post. The two inhabitants looked up, shocked, taken completely by surprise. Before they could reposition and fire the Spandau, Herb released two quick bursts of his Tommy gun. The Germans fell back into their pit, one mortally wounded and clutching at the air, the other crumpled dead into a corner.

Herb crouched low as another Spandau opened up at him. He spun, dug his feet into the sand, and sprinted in zigzag fashion towards the gunners' nest. Once again, his speed and unpredictability caught the Germans off guard. Bullets whizzed by him as he dived headlong under the rim of the pit. Placing his Tommy gun to his shoulder he sprayed bullets into the gun pit, killing the two occupants instantly.

Where was the rest of the company? Why was no one else firing? A quick look behind revealed the shocking truth. Herb was alone. Nobody was following. There was no one able to follow.

He was the last man standing.

Flares irradiated the scene again. Herb suddenly realised he was very vulnerable and isolated. He dived into the pit of the machine-gun post he had just cleaned out. All he could see out in front of him were square helmets.

He inched over the parapet of the pit and fired a few shots. He was rewarded by seeing two Germans fall. He ducked back in as bullets whistled over the top of his hole. Some thumped into the sandbags around the rim. The enemy was everywhere. He waited till the flares died down, then put his head up and fired at some more shadowy figures. A scream and a German expletive filled the air. In the dark, Herb was still deadly.

A few minutes later, he attempted to shoot over the parapet again. This time, his Tommy gun jammed. Damn. He knew the weapon intimately and quickly dismantled it. Finding the problem, he rebuilt the gun and continued his personal and lonely war.

Astoundingly, he noticed that some of the Germans were moving away. His persistence, accuracy and rate of fire were still making a difference. But it wasn't enough. He could see that they were effectively all around him. Eventually he realised there was no way he could handle this by himself. He'd better get out.

He waited until the flares settled. When he was sure it was dark enough, he sprang to his feet, then sprinted. He had only pounded out a few metres when the flares exploded into the night sky again. Herb was lit up like a beacon, caught like a rabbit in the headlights.

'No!' He cursed to himself. He was sure every German rifleman and machine gunner on the Ring Contour would see him. And they did. A tremendous salvo from a vengeful enemy raked across the vicinity of Herb's fleeing form. The flames from a multitude of weapons sparkled from defensive positions on the Ring Contour. Herb could hear bullets zipping around him, whizzing between his legs and thudding into the desert floor. Some were tracers and skidded past him like long-tailed meteors.

His legs moved even faster. They carried him back to where he had initiated his charge. He ran over a rise and fell over a body lying prone. He rolled instinctively, sat up and aimed his gun.

'Who's that?'

'It's me, Herb, Blondie Gwynne. Geez mate. How many bloody holes have you got in you?'

Herb said, 'I don't think I'm hit.'

'Bullshit,' Gwynne replied, 'I've seen 'em going through you. I saw the tracers race all around you—through your legs—everywhere!'

Herb rolled over and examined himself.

'Nope, I must be lucky. I'm not hit.'

Herb picked up Gwynne and began to help him back, moving a little out of range.

Herb said, 'I'll go and help some other wounded. There must be a lot of them out there because nobody followed me. Can you walk okay now?'

'Yes, I'll manage.'

The two men had only been searching for a few minutes when they stumbled across ten Germans, all wounded, lying on the ground. They were all in a bad way. Most were bandaged. There was blood everywhere and they were waiting for assistance. They had had enough. The senior officer, with his hands up, approached Herb. In perfect English he said, 'Do not shoot me. I'm Jesus Christ.'

Herb allowed himself a wry smile, then took them all prisoner. He assisted them to their feet and directed them back towards the Eighth Army lines. Such was the tension of the moment that it took a few moments for Gwynne to realise that the German had spoken English. 'You know, Herb, that Jerry spoke perfect English.' It amused them both.

Along the way, the men found Lieutenant Treloar, commander of 18 Platoon, needing assistance with his smashed leg, as well as Herb's mate, Norm Leaney, also coping with a broken leg.

Emerging from the darkness, Herb heard another distinctly Australian voice. It was 'Froggy' Deceau from his 17 Platoon. Wounded in the stomach himself, Deceau was escorting four wounded Germans, marching behind and hitting them with a trench shovel. He was angry and belted each on the head in turn. The pantomime had an element of macabre humour repudiated by Deceau's admonishments. 'You bastards killed all my mates . . .'

Unfortunately, the tension escalated and in the darkened half-light of the early dawn, one prisoner, an officer, produced a pistol. He aimed it at Deceau and fired. The bullet went through the lobe of Deceau's ear. Deceau angrily recoiled, blood spurting from his ear. 'You can't put a bullet through my ear. I'll teach you a lesson. You're a prisoner. You aren't supposed to do that!' His indignant comments caused some mirth among the Australians, but Deceau's justice was abrupt, final and not at all humorous. Deceau raised his own rifle, pressed the butt into his shoulder and shot the prisoner through the heart. The German dropped instantly to the ground, dead.

The group joined Herb's party. As they moved back, they found eight more wounded German soldiers keen to surrender. They also came across several other wounded men from D Company. Herb directed the Germans to assist in carrying out the injured men and then insisted that other Germans lead the way. They were bordering a minefield and he hoped they knew a safe route.

They would yell, 'Mines, mines . . . there, there!' Herb and the entourage followed, treading very carefully.

Eventually, after tensely weaving through the minefield, the tattered looking group reached the Blockhouse. Only three men from D Company were walking unaided—sixteen had been killed, the rest wounded. They had brought in 21 prisoners.

Earlier, there had been a strong battle for the Blockhouse. The Blockhouse was a pre-war railway ganger's hut, and had more recently been used as a German hospital. It was built of grey concrete and contained six rooms, all interconnected, and had been overtaken by the 2/32nd Battalion. The battalion medical officer, Dr Bill Campbell, worked alongside Captain Grice, the medical officer from 2/11 Field Ambulance, three captured German medical officers and nine orderlies. Together they treated men from both armies. Now, they were joined by Dr Guy Robertson, the medical officer from the 2/24th Battalion, and Dr Yeatman from the 2/48th Battalion. Here, the medical team collaborated in an enlightened gesture of international unity.

When Herb arrived with his group of prisoners, Dr Robertson came out to inspect them. He was most relieved to see Herb in charge. He laughed, 'Thank God it's you. We can't always tell what's going on outside. We just hear the gunfire and we don't know who's winning. I didn't know whether we'd be going to Germany or not. I'll go back in and tell my German colleagues they are still our prisoners.'

As dawn was breaking, Herb left his collection of wounded men in the doctors' care and walked over to meet the remainder of the battalion. Battalion Headquarters had been set up in the Saucer, east of Barrel Hill. He found that Hammer had been wounded, shot through the cheek, and the other three companies had also been devastated. Of the 213 men of the 2/48th Battalion who had gone into battle the previous evening, only 41 were left standing. That grievous night, they had taken over 200 German prisoners. The figures were numbing. After what he had just experienced, the loss was almost too profound for Herb to comprehend.

The remainder of the 2/24th Battalion were also recovering from their ordeal. They were dug in to the left of the Saucer, next to the 2/32nd Battalion. They had been halted several hundred metres from Thompson's Post, their objective. Their attrition rate had also been intolerable: they were left with only 74 men, losing 42 killed and 116 wounded.

The killing wasn't over for the night. Herb had no sooner reported to headquarters when he noticed four German soldiers about 200 metres away standing on a raised section of the railway line. They were obviously preparing to give themselves up and had their hands high in the air, their square helmets clearly distinguishable in the early morning light. Suddenly, the unmistakable rattle of a Spandau cut the air. Herb braced, and then was shocked to see the four Germans crash to the ground, cut to pieces by the murderous fire. 'Crikey. The bastards have killed their own men.'

The assassin was firing from the other side of the railway line, about 50 metres from the hapless soldiers, and could hardly have missed. Herb reacted quickly. The embankment here was about 2 metres high. He grabbed a nearby soldier and the two of them stealthily crept along the near slope of the embankment, keeping out of sight of the German gunman on the other side.

They then climbed the embankment, crouching low, and carefully negotiated the railway tracks to come out behind the German. Herb gave a short burst of his Tommy gun and the executioner fell dead over his Spandau.

Herb returned to the battalion and, with the other 40 members, dug in and prepared to defend Barrel Hill. Next to them was the 2/32nd Battalion and further over the remnants of the 2/24th Battalion—about 200 men in all. The 2/3rd Pioneer Battalion, who had thrust deep towards the coast the previous evening, also withdrew to positions around Barrel Hill. The four depleted battalions prepared to hold the line against a smarting and desperate enemy—a very thin line.

They did not have long to wait. Rommel, who had been considering retreating, changed his tack. He charged the Afrika Korps commander, General von Thoma, to attack with his powerful 21st Panzer Division and the 90th Light Infantry. As the morning light strengthened, Herb could see the intimidating spectacle of twenty heavy Mark III tanks and one Mark IV heading right for the 2/48th Battalion's positions. And right behind were the German infantry. To his relief, the 'cavalry' saved the day, 32 Valentine tanks from the 40th Royal Tank Regiment arriving on cue to meet them. The Saucer and the area around it was about to became the hottest spot on the El Alamein line. Everybody was aware that if the Germans broke through now, it could be critical for the whole campaign.

A number of the British tanks raced up to the larger Tigers and opened fire at close range, assisted by consistent pounding from the

Australian 2/3rd Anti-Tank Regiment and a Rhodesian Anti-Tank Battery. The battle was played out right in front of the 2/48th, and the battalion came under heavy fire from 88-mm and anti-tank shells all day.

Herb watched with admiration as the smaller Valentines harassed their stronger counterparts, even though they were outgunned and had less armour. The conflict went on for a desperate seven hours, with the sounds of exploding tanks, the whine of shells and the crash of guns reverberating around the Saucer.

Herb crouched deep in his trench, once again cursing his vulnerability; he had no corrugated iron to cover him this time. Along with his exhausted 2/48th companions lying in trenches, his battalion continued to suffer casualties. A direct hit from an 88-mm shell killed the battalion adjutant, Captain Bill Reid, while the commanding officer of C Company, Captain Mick Bryant, was also wounded.

But nothing could detract from the courage of the Valentine tank commanders. They lost 22 tanks along with 44 crewmen dead for the prize of eight Tigers—enough pressure to turn the Germans back. There would be no German breakout that day. By late afternoon, however, it was becoming obvious to Morshead just how debilitated his forces at the Saucer had become. He understood that Rommel would still be in an aggressive mood the next day, and that he would need fresh troops to hold him. He issued orders at 7.30 that evening that two of the 26th Brigade battalions, the 2/24th and 2/48th, would be relieved. These two sister battalions, bonded in blood, had lost more than 400 men between them. The 2/32nd and 2/3rd Pioneers would remain.

The 2/48th would be replaced by the 2/43rd Battalion. This battalion had seen some action on the first night of the battle, but was otherwise fresh, seasoned and fit. The convoy arrived late in the evening and drove straight up to the railway, guides leading the trucks over the lines and then across to the Saucer. Here they found the dilapidated remains of the 2/48th Battalion. The sight obviously distressed them, one soldier saying to Herb, 'My God. Look at you. Where's the rest of the battalion?'

Herb replied, 'You're looking at it!'

The relief was more than welcome. The exhausted members of the 2/48th walked to the pickup line and were amused to count 40 troop carriers lined up ready to transport both 2/24th and 2/48th out of the battle area. The commander of the truck drivers asked Herb the same question. 'Where's your battalion?'

'This is all there is.'

The driver shook his head incredulously. Only two troop carriers were needed to drive them back to the 'cutting' area at Tel el Eisa. Once safely in the trucks and out of the firing line, some men broke down. A few sobbed, some shook uncontrollably. It was late, close to 2.00 a.m., when they arrived at their campsite and were offered a hot meal. No one spoke. Most actions were mechanical.

The food was tasty enough but Herb ate it uncaringly, staring distractedly into his mug of tea. He turned in, but sleep was not easy. Like most of his friends, he lay in his trench and silently gazed into the crystal black void above El Alamein. He threw unanswerable questions into the depths of the firmament; he was too numb to be angry or to attempt to understand. An individual soldier in a vast army does not immediately see the benefits or reasons for his actions. Thoughts spun in his mind, searching for order. Violent and regrettable experiences had been seared into the recesses of his memory; the events of this night would be indelibly etched. Herb would never forget El Alamein. Like his companions, he had seen too much death and killing. For what point, he would not know until later. However, one thing was for sure—his character, forged in a crucible of fire, had been taught to endure. He would need this knowledge. For the battle, and the war, was not over.

But for now at least, events had conspired to grant Herb an all too brief respite. Earlier that day, on the morning of 31 October, Montgomery had agreed to postpone Supercharge until the following evening—the night of 1 November.

FIFTEEN

The Breakout

A t first light on 1 November, the struggle at the Saucer escalated, reflecting Rommel's strong intention to regain it. As
the bleary-eyed and exhausted soldiers of the 2/48th Battalion
were lining up for their morning roll call, the sound of battle
echoed across from the positions they had vacated the previous
evening. Smoke, dust and flashes from exploding bombs highlighted the degree of aggression that the incumbent battalions
were receiving.

Enemy pressure mounted against these units throughout
the day with small-arms fire, mortars and 88-mm guns firing
airbursts and field guns blasting their positions. Two German
divisions struck hard at the Australians. Overhead, Stukas
joined in the fray and dogfights took place as they were intercepted by the Desert Air Force fighters. The Stukas were no
match for the Kittyhawks and all were shot down before they
could do much damage. Red tracer shells spurted up like ruby
necklaces. Against this assault, the Australians held the line.

In the meantime, Herb was shocked as the roll call that
morning revealed the full extent of the losses incurred by the
2/48th Battalion. Herb was still acting commander of D
Company and only a dozen of his men were able to answer the
call. The final tally confirmed 41 from the battalion in atten-
dance that morning. For those survivors, there was a strong

sense of pride in the battalion's achievements, but it was over-shadowed by a profound sense of loss and sorrow. These few days' respite would be important.

Over at the Saucer, the attrition continued. Desert Air Force Boston bombers rained havoc, pattern-bombing enemy targets, their familiar 'football team' clusters of eighteen aircraft hovering serenely above the smoke of battle. At dusk, German tanks pushed at the positions and were repulsed. The members of the 2/48th Battalion were now very aware that if they had not been pulled out, they would surely have been completely wiped out.

Morshead's gamble to replace the depleted battalions had paid off. It was always going to be a risk attempting the changeover amid such turmoil, but it was important that fit battalions were ready for the enemy. The pressure from both sides continued into the evening, but time was running out for Rommel.

British tanks had been moving up behind the 9th Division to begin Supercharge, wallowing and churning up knee-deep dust, inadvertently cutting off all communication lines to the Saucer and the 9th Division. They were preparing for the breakout.

At 1.05 a.m. on 2 November, an intense artillery barrage south of the Australians announced the opening of Operation Supercharge. By morning, 120 Sherman tanks, each one 30 tons of hardened steel, had passed through the gap just south of Trig 29 to meet the German behemoths. The breakout was at hand.

In the meantime, back at Tel el Eisa, Herb and his troop had a minor windfall. The first beer was delivered to the battalion and a Naafi supply truck approached D Company.

'Who's in charge?' the driver asked.

'I am,' said Herb.

'What strength have you got there?'

'Full company strength—120 men.'

The driver didn't query him and Herb helped unload ten dozen bottles. Should be good, thought Herb. About ten bottles a man—that's fair.

Herb thanked the driver and watched him negotiate his way back to the main road. A few minutes later, an explosion, followed by the sound of tinkling glass, interrupted the relative peace of Herb's morning. The truck had run over a mine, blowing off its back wheel. The remaining bottles crashed off the truck, the beer soaking into the desert sand. Fortunately, the driver was uninjured, though shaken—Herb suspected as much for the loss of the amber fluid as for the near miss.

The beer was greatly appreciated by the men of D Company, sustaining them for the next few days.

In the meantime, further south, the Allied tanks and infantry had pushed an opening into enemy territory 5.5 kilometres deep and 3.5 kilometres wide, sprawling towards Tel el Aqqaqir. Here they were engaged by 120 Italian and German tanks in a life-and-death struggle in the heat of the midday sun. Across the desert, pitched tank battles were fought in scenes defying description. In one great thrust, the 9th Armoured (tank) Brigade pushed the enemy back a further 2 kilometres. It was at a heavy price, however, the brigade losing 112 of its 132 tanks. But Rommel was desperate now. He too had lost many tanks, and in addition was low on fuel and ammunition. He realised he would have to retreat.

On 3 November, the final breakthrough set the desert aflame. Literally hundreds of Allied tanks poured through the gap, fanning in all directions, intent only on pushing the enemy backwards. Clashes with German and Italian tanks, infantry, artillery and planes ignited a broad landscape of epic battle. Scenes of horror and heroism were enacted in equal measure. All day, sounds of one of the most desperate conflicts of the desert campaign filtered back to the men at Tel el Eisa.

On 4 November, a large element—about 80 men of the 2/48th, including Herb and those wounded now fit for action— were detached back to Trig 29. By now, the intensity of the fighting in that area had settled.

The same day, the battalion received a visit from Lieutenant-General Montgomery. He and General Alexander had just left Lieutenant-General Morshead's headquarters to express their appreciation of the 9th Division's role in the victory.

Monty was wearing his slouch hat and was in high spirits. Herb was impressed by his easygoing manner and noted how relaxed he was around the Australians. He had come over particularly to congratulate the battalion on their magnificent effort. Even though he was mainly engaged with Lieutenant-Colonel Hammer, he was extremely accessible, encouraging Herb and others to speak.

There had been tank battles raging for some days, but Montgomery said, 'Now the tanks are out, we should win the show from here.'

He had always made it clear he didn't want to just push Rommel back, he wanted to annihilate him. He may well have been inspired by an iconic British military dictate of Nelson as he paced the quarterdeck of *Victory* one and a half centuries earlier. Before the Battle of Trafalgar, Nelson was quoted as saying, 'It is annihilation that the country wants, not merely a splendid victory.'

Montgomery said, 'If you look out there,' pointing westward, 'in about an hour or so you'll witness the largest tank battle you'll ever see in your life.'

Over the previous few days, 60000 troops and thousands of vehicles, trucks and tanks had breached the minefield. Titanic battles had already taken place, although this would be the largest and most chaotic. Herb watched in awe as hundreds of tanks wheeled and roared, crashed, exploded and burned.

The desert, quivering in the haze, transformed into a scene from hell; a confused arena clouded by bursts of high explosives, darkened by smoke, lit by flashes of innumerable guns, heightened by red, green and white tracers, shaken by heavy aerial bombing and deafened by the artillery of both sides. The Desert Air Force grabbed its share. Hurricanes, equipped with large-calibre guns, dived into the melee and dealt death to tanks in sudden violent raids. It was obvious to Herb why the Hurricanes were dubbed 'the tin openers'.

Through all this, two Allied armoured divisions and an Italian armoured division clubbed at each other, while further south at Tel el Aqqaqir, not far from Herb, another Allied armoured division threshed at the German tanks.

Eventually, tanks finally ground to a halt and the tenuous Axis defence collapsed. The spectre of defeat for Rommel hung over the battlefield. Another major coup occurred about midday as the commander of the German Afrika Korps, General von Thoma, was captured. He was found standing by his destroyed tank, the last of his squadron. By late afternoon, the enemy was in full retreat.

In Herb's local area, the battle at the Saucer and surrounding area had already been won. The Cloverleaf had been occupied by the 26th Brigade, and the surrounding area opened up. The main road had been cleared of mines and more traffic began to move westward.

The fighting around Thompson's Post had stopped, but it was not clear whether the enemy had retreated as the post had never been captured. Hammer approached Herb. The wounds in his cheeks from the 31 October fight were scarcely visible. Amazingly, the German bullet which had pierced his cheek and exited through the other had not touched a bone or tooth. 'Sergeant Ashby,' he said, 'take another man and check out Thompson's Post. No one is moving; we suspect they've left.'

'Yes, sir.' Herb had great respect for Hammer. His orders were always direct, and even though it was broad daylight and he had reason to be nervous, he trusted Hammer's judgement. He knew Hammer would never ask anything of any soldier that he would not be prepared to attempt himself.

Herb seconded Frank Smith and they tentatively approached Thompson's Post. The word 'post' was misleading. Lieutenant John Thompson of the 2/17th Battalion had led a patrol there in mid-August and confirmed a large enemy presence. There were numerous defensive positions in the immediate vicinity, creating a potentially powerful situation. And Herb was about to enter it.

As they got closer, Herb and Smith crawled on their bellies to within 100 metres of the post. While they contemplated their situation, Herb said to Smith, with a half-grin, 'Have you ever thought about Germany?'

'Why?'

'Well, if there are Germans still there, we'll be going on a holiday there shortly.' They both laughed. Even though they made light of the situation, Herb had made up his mind that if the place was still strongly occupied, he would surrender. They were only two men and it would have been crazy to fight. As they entered the enemy's territory, they were repelled by a strong stench of rotting bodies and death. Battered and burnt-out tanks emphasised the ferocity of the final armoured clashes. Dead soldiers littered the area, some hanging grotesquely out of the hulls of tanks, most blackened and forced into bizarre postures by pain in their dying moments. They found some Australians from the 2/24th lying sprawled among their enemy, both sides united in death.

Just in time, Herb noticed a trip wire running between two large bombs. The area was booby trapped! 'F' Christ's sake, look where you're walking,' he yelled. This was still a dangerous area.

As he passed a dead German officer, Herb noticed a beautiful pair of precision Zeiss binoculars around his neck. Herb helped himself, and relieved the man of his weapon too—a prized Luger pistol. Content that there was no one alive and the area was safe to be occupied, Herb and Smith started moving back towards their battalion.

As they walked away they noticed men from other units approaching the site from several directions. Herb realised they had been observed by other battalions who were waiting to see if it was safe to go in. Herb laughed. 'Looks like we're definitely the first to go in. The buggers were just waiting for us to check it out.'

Hammer was watching them also from Battalion Headquarters on Trig 29. When Herb returned, the colonel congratulated him.

'Thanks Colonel. They must have shot through when they saw us coming,' Herb quipped.

That evening, Rommel was clearly aware that he was in danger of encirclement. At 5.30 p.m., even though some of his troops were already in full flight, he authorised a retreat to begin immediately.

The Battle of El Alamein was won.

Next day, 5 November, while the battle swirled around the Axis lines and tanks and lorries continued to stream past the men on Trig 29, Herb joined official burial parties at Ring Contour 25. He had been requested to travel with Padre Archbold to follow the track where D Company had fought on the night of 30 October. The area was still littered with dead men, bodies of both Germans and Australians strewn at random. Some had been buried in makeshift graves by the Germans after the bitter fighting on that night.

During the search, Herb walked over a soft piece of depressed earth. He dug down and found 35 men buried in what was a large bomb hole. Herb sorted the ones he knew and recorded them, particularly the men from his platoon. It was sad work, but eventually he found them all. (These men were later re-interned at the brigade cemetery at El Alamein.) Herb then organised for the men's personal effects to be forwarded to their next of kin.

That evening, at Trig 29, Herb could see long columns of Allied trucks and vehicles filled with troops racing towards Libya. In the air above, Desert Air Force planes reported massive columns of enemy vehicles fleeing westwards, nose to tail, creating marvellous targets for them. An army in retreat is a sad sight. The chase was well and truly on.

Later that night, hundreds of fires lit up the desert as burnt-out hulks of tanks and other vehicles told the story. By that afternoon, word had filtered through to the Australians that Rommel had not only withdrawn but was in full flight. He had been given no choice but to abandon the bulk of the Italian infantry; there were no transports or fuel. Only relatively few men from the eight Italian divisions managed to get away; the rest were lost—well over 20000 men. At the same time, 10000 Germans were taken prisoner.

As well, his armoured units were virtually destroyed. By the time Rommel had left Mersa Matruh three days later, he escaped with only about a dozen German tanks—450 of them were left at El Alamein. The Italian tank contingent fared a little better, escaping with about 100 of their original 290.

News that thousands of Germans and Italians had surrendered created a feeling of euphoria. The Australians had found many flares of all kinds while 'scrounging' and 'souveniring' in the enemy's abandoned positions, and after one or two were fired it triggered a spontaneous Guy Fawkes Day fireworks celebration.

Exactly 337 years earlier, Guy Fawkes was arrested as he prepared to commit what would have been the greatest single act of political and religious terrorism in English history by attempting to blow up the House of Lords. Herb recalled the rhyme:

Remember, remember, the fifth of November,
Gunpowder treason and plot.
We see no reason,
Why gunpowder treason,
Should ever be forgot.

The date and ditty would forever remind the men of the Eighth Army of the victory at El Alamein.

That was the end of the Battle of El Alamein for the men of the 9th Division. The pursuit of Rommel was taken up by the remaining elements of the Eighth Army, who would be joined by the Americans and other British troops on 8 November in landings in northwest Africa in an operation codenamed Torch, aimed to catch the Afrika Korps in a 'pincer' movement.

Over the next few days, as there were no officers left, Herb wrote individual letters to the next of kin of the deceased members of his platoon. He would attempt to comfort the recipient by relaying the sadness felt by him personally and also by the platoon. He would write about the importance of the work the soldier had been doing and praise his efforts in the context of the campaign, and maybe add a personal anecdote or two. It was one of the most difficult tasks ever required of him.

He also approached the adjutant in order to honour Captain Robbins's request to recommend an award for Bill Kibby. Robbins had actually left a note in his uniform to that effect which was found when his body was discovered. The content advised of his desire to recommend Kibby for a DCM for his bravery on the night of the 25th. As it was not possible to be awarded a DCM posthumously, the only awards available were either the Victoria Cross or MID (Mentioned in Dispatches). Once again, as Herb was not an officer, he and two privates were interviewed by the adjutant who authorised the request.

The battalion stayed in the Tel el Eisa area for the next month. Here they rested, cleaned up, swam in the Mediterranean, talked or silently reflected, and generally recuperated. Most tried to come to terms with the devastating experiences they had been through. For some, it was difficult to reconcile their losses as the only other 9th Division battalion to lose more men was their sister battalion, the 2/24th.

Congratulations soon began to pour in from dignitaries, politicians and military leaders alike, heralding the 9th Division's role in the battle as not only integral to the overall success, but actually pivotal. On 15 November, church bells rang in Britain for the first time since 1940, in celebration of the victory in Egypt. For the men of the 9th Division, there was now a deep feeling of pride that they had been tested and had risen gallantly to the occasion.

On 3 December, as part of twelve mammoth convoys transporting the 9th Division, the battalion retraced the original journey which brought them to Egypt from Palestine. Three days later they set up camp at Beit Jirja, not far from their original campsite of Camp Julis, midway between Gaza and Tel Aviv.

At this stage, Herb was asked if he would like to attend OCTU (Officer Cadet Training Unit) to become an officer. Herb was flattered, but he declined. Inwardly, he felt his lack of higher education would let him down, although later he realised he probably could have made it. The other men who did attend were surprised the course lasted for only three weeks rather than the usual three months. However, it didn't really bother Herb. Attaining rank wasn't high on his list of priorities.

In the meantime, new winter dress clothing was issued and men started betting on whether they would be returning to Australia soon. On 12 December, the colonel received orders to train his men for a large ceremonial parade to be held at Gaza airport just before Christmas. The whole 9th Division would assemble for the first time and march in review. The salute was to be taken by Commander-in-Chief, Middle East, General Sir Harold Alexander. It was an opportunity for the Australians to show how they could train to the highest order of precision marching and display exemplary arms drill in addition to acquitting themselves steadfastly in battle.

On 22 December, the parade assembled, stretching for more than a kilometre and creating a most impressive spectacle. The background scene of green fields provided a marvellous contrast to the burnt and desolate desert landscape that the men had grown used to. After Alexander's address, there was an emotional yet disciplined salute to fallen comrades. The whole division—over 12 000 men—came to the general salute in perfect unison. They then stood motionless in the present arms stance as the general carried out his long inspection, remaining at the salute while standing in the back of an open and moving car.

Then, with great pride, in close columns by companies, the whole division marched 40 abreast to salute General Alexander. The day was a most memorable event to Herb. They had marched and performed brilliantly; it was something to be proud of.

To Herb, the parade was a chance to pay tribute to the heavy losses incurred during the battle. Between July and November, the division had lost 1225 men killed at El Alamein, 620 of them in the final twelve days.

Alexander's words would echo back at Herb forever. 'Your reputations as fighters has always been famous,' he said, 'but I do not believe that you have ever fought with greater bravery or distinction than you did during that battle when you broke the German and Italian armies in the Western Desert. Now you have added fresh lustre to your already illustrious name.'

* * *

The battalion stayed on in Palestine for another month. When, on the morning of 23 January 1943, they moved out towards Suez, there was no doubt in everybody's minds they would be heading home. That same morning, they also heard news that the Eighth Army had entered Tripoli, the capital of Libya. Rommel was fast approaching his nemesis.

Two days later, with the rest of the 26th Brigade, they were camped at Port Tewfik on the east bank of the Suez Canal waiting their turn to board the return convoy to Australia, when an announcement came through from a headquarters official of the decorations gained during the El Alamein battle. Herb and his 17 Platoon friends were thrilled to hear Sergeant Bill Kibby was posthumously awarded the Victoria Cross—the second for their platoon. The battalion won another posthumous Victoria Cross during the battle, awarded to Private Percy Gratwick. Captain Robbins was awarded an MID and Captain Zac Isaksson of the carrier platoon a Military Cross. There were many others too; the battalion was covered in glory.

On 1 February, the battalion boarded the *Nieuw Amsterdam*, a magnificent Dutch liner. As the ship moved down the Red Sea towards the coast of Eritrea, she was joined by four other monarchs of the sea and, in convoy, headed back to Australia, leaving the Desert Campaign far behind.

A few days out to sea, Herb was interviewed by the colonel and posted as a confirmed sergeant. He still had two years of war to go.

The official British report on the Battle of El Alamein states: 'The 9th Australian Division put up a magnificent effort. They fought themselves and the enemy to a standstill, till flesh and blood could stand no more. Then they went on fighting'.

The Years After

The 2/48th Battalion continued to fight through many campaigns against the Japanese in New Guinea and the Pacific Islands. The unit, with four Victoria Crosses and 96 other decorations, become the most decorated battalion of the AIF in the Second World War, fighting from Tobruk to Tarakan.

Here's what happened to some of the characters of the battalion.

Herb Ashby

Herb took part in all the Pacific campaigns except for Tarakan, the final one. He was discharged in May 1945 with war-related diseases before the war in the Pacific finished. While he was repatriating in Mount Gambier Hospital he met a nurse, Heather Hancock, whom he married later that year. Upon discharge, he helped his uncle to manage a property called OB Flat, about 10 kilometres from Mount Gambier, until 1948.

Eventually, he was awarded a soldier settlement property at Mingbool, 16 kilometres from Mount Gambier. He commenced farming and built up a dairy herd of 100 cows. Then he added sheep, fat lambs and beef cattle, and expanded by buying another property over the road.

Herb did well with this investment and lifestyle before selling up in the mid-1970s to live in Mount Gambier. He had used irrigation on his property and had learned about water resources over the years, so he landed a good job as an inspector of water resources. Eventually, he became responsible for underground water in the southeast corner of the state, remaining in this position until he retired in the mid-1980s. In the meantime, he had also built some apartments, which kept him interested and busy. It was a life he enjoyed.

Since 1946, he had been a pensions officer for ex-servicemen and widows, assisting them to apply for pensions from the Department of Veterans' Affairs; some men were too sick or too traumatised to help themselves. He also did a great deal of Legacy and RSL work, and continues to do so today. In 1999, he was awarded a Medal of the Order of Australia (OAM) for this work, bringing his tally of medals to a dozen.

Herb celebrated his 60th wedding anniversary to Heather in 2005. Together they have five adult children, eight grandchildren and six great-grandchildren. They still live in Mount Gambier where Herb continues to take an active interest in the RSL (December 2005).

Tom 'Diver' Derrick, VC, DCM

'Diver' continued with the battalion to New Guinea and won a brilliant Victoria Cross at Sattelburg in November 1943. Although he was entitled to retire from active fighting, he continued to lead his platoon through to Tarakan. Here he was killed by a burst of machine-gun fire on 23 May 1945.

'Blondie' Gwynne

'Blondie' returned to Western Australia after the war and is now retired in Perth.

Zac Isaksson

After the war, until 1948, Zac was part of the Occupational Forces in Japan with 66 Battalion, a unit put together from the 9th Division. He joined the Regular Army and rose to the rank of brigadier, spending time in Canberra as deputy director of Joint Intelligence Organisation until 1971. He resigned and worked with Ciba-Geigy for eight years, then he and his wife bought and worked an avocado farm at Mapleton in Queensland for 25 years. In 2003 he retired and now lives in Sydney.

Norm Leaney

Norm returned to Adelaide and was very active all his life in the Battalion Association. He died in the early 2000s.

'Lofty' Whaite

'Lofty' returned to Port Lincoln in South Australia after the war. He became mayor of the town in the 1950s and died in the 1970s.

Further Reading

Badman, P., *North Africa 1940–42: The Desert War*, Time-Life Books, Sydney, 1998

Carver, M., *El Alamein*, Wordsworth Editions, Hertfordshire, UK, 1962

Collier, R., *The War in the Desert*, Time-Life Books, Alexandria, VA, USA, 1977

Cousins, W.H.E., *The Siege of Tobruk: An overview*, The Rats of Tobruk Assoc. Aust., Redcliffe, QLD, 1999

Farquhar, M., *Derrick VC*, Rigby Publishers, Adelaide, 1982

Glenn, J.G., *Tobruk to Tarakan*, Rigby Limited, Adelaide, 1960

Goodman, R., *I was a Rat: Tobruk, 1941*, Copyright Publishing Company, Brisbane, 2004

Johnston, M., *That Magnificent 9th*, Allen & Unwin, Sydney, 2002

Johnston, M. and Stanley, P., *Alamein: The Australian Story*, Oxford University Press, Melbourne, 2002

Khaki and Green, Australian War Memorial, Canberra, 1943

Maughan, B., *Tobruk and El Alamein*, Collins with the Australian War Memorial, Canberra, 1987

Oakes, B., *Muzzle Blast, 2/2nd Machine Gun Battalion*, Sydney, 1980

Share, P., *Mud and Blood*, Heritage Book Publications, Frankston, Vic, 1978

'Silver John', *Target Tank*, self-published, Parramatta, 1957